THE ECONOMICS
OF DISCRETIONARY BEHAVIOR:
MANAGERIAL OBJECTIVES
IN A THEORY OF THE FIRM

THE ECONOMICS

OF DISCRETIONARY BEHAVIOR:

MANAGERIAL OBJECTIVES

IN A THEORY OF THE FIRM

OLIVER E. WILLIAMSON

Assistant Professor
of Economics
University of California,
Berkeley

PRENTICE-HALL, INC.

Englewood Cliffs, N.J.

1960 Award Winners

Bernard H. Baum *Decentralization of Authority in a Bureaucracy*
Dissertation submitted to Department of Sociology, University of Chicago

Leon V. Hirsch *Marketing in an Underdeveloped Economy: The North Indian Sugar Industry*
Dissertation submitted to Graduate School of Business Administration, Harvard University

Bedros Peter Pashigian *The Distribution of Automobiles, an Economic Analysis of the Franchise System*
Dissertation submitted to Department of Economics, Massachusetts Institute of Technology

Martin Patchen *The Choice of Wage Comparison*
Dissertation submitted to Department of Social Psychology, University of Michigan

Fred M. Tonge *A Heuristic Program for Assembly Line Balancing*
Dissertation submitted to Graduate School of Industrial Administration, Carnegie Institute of Technology

1959 Award Winners

Kalman J. Cohen *Computer Models of the Shoe, Leather, Hide Sequence*
Dissertation submitted to Graduate School of Industrial Administration, Carnegie Institute of Technology

Bob R. Holdren *The Structure of a Retail Market and the Market Behavior of Retail Units*
Dissertation submitted to Department of Economics, Yale University

Frank Proschan *Polya Type Distributions in Renewal Theory, with an Application to an Inventory Problem*
Dissertation submitted to Department of Statistics, Stanford University

Andrew C. Stedry *Budget Control and Cost Behavior*
Dissertation submitted to Graduate School of Industrial Administration, Carnegie Institute of Technology

Victor H. Vroom *Some Personality Determinants of the Effects of Participation*
Dissertation submitted to Department of Psychology, University of Michigan

1962 Award Winners

Alexander Barges *The Effect of Capital Structure on the Cost of Capital*
Dissertation submitted to Graduate School of Business Administration, Northwestern University

Charles P. Bonini *Simulation of Information and Decision Systems in the Firm*
Dissertation submitted to Graduate School of Business, Carnegie Institute of Technology

James M. Ferguson *The Advertising Rate Structure in the Daily Newspaper Industry*
Dissertation submitted to Department of Economics, University of Chicago

Gordon M. Kaufman *Statistical Decision and Related Techniques in Oil and Gas Exploration*
Dissertation submitted to Graduate School of Business, Harvard University

H. Martin Weingartner *Mathematical Programming and the Analysis of Capitaʾ Budgeting Problems*
Dissertation submitted to Graduate School of Industrial Administration, Carnegie Institute of Technology

1961 Award Winners

Geoffrey P. E. Clarkson *Portfolio Selection: A Simulation of Trust Investment*
Dissertation submitted to Graduate School of Industrial Administration, Carnegie Institute of Technology

Donald E. Farrar *The Investment Decision Under Uncertainty: Portfolio Selection*
Dissertation submitted to Faculty of Arts and Sciences, Harvard University

Richard S. Hatch *An Evaluation of a Forced-Choice Differential Accuracy Approach to the Measurement of Supervisory Empathy*
Dissertation submitted to Department of Psychology, University of Minnesota

David Meiselman *The Term Structure of Interest Rates*
Dissertation submitted to Department of Economics, University of Chicago

George William Summers *Financing and Initial Operations of New Firms*
Dissertation submitted to Department of Management, Case Institute of Technology

Foreword

Dr. Williamson's dissertation, completed during the academic year 1962–1963, is one of six selected for publication in the fifth annual Doctoral Dissertation Competition sponsored by the Program in Economic Development and Administration of the Ford Foundation.

The intent of the doctoral dissertation competition has been to recognize and encourage excellence in research on business by graduate students. Publication awards, now totaling twenty-six, have been made over the five years of the competition to persons granted doctorates in business and related fields whose thesis research on problems of business was especially distinguished by its analytical content and strong roots in the underlying disciplines common to business.

In addition to Dr. Williamson's, the dissertations published this year are:

The Demand for Liquid Assets: A Temporal Cross-Section Analysis
  Edgar Louis Feige
  Department of Economics
  University of Chicago

An Evaluation of Level of Aspiration As a Training Procedure
  Forrest W. Fryer
  Department of Psychology
  University of Maryland

The Demand for Physical Capital: Application of a Wealth Model
  Frederick S. Hammer
  Graduate School of Industrial Administration
  Carnegie Institute of Technology

The Measurement of Cumulative Advertising Effects
  Kristian S. Palda
  Graduate School of Business
  University of Chicago

Some Large-Scale Production Scheduling Problems in the Paper Industry
> John F. Pierce, Jr.
> School of Industrial Management
> Massachusetts Institute of Technology

On behalf of the Ford Foundation, I wish to express my gratitude to the members of the Editorial Committee for the care and thought they devoted to the selection process. The members of this Committee, who made the final selection of winning dissertations, were: Professor Robert Ferber of the University of Illinois, Professor Mason Haire of the University of California at Berkeley, and Professor Thomas L. Whisler of the University of Chicago

The Editorial Committee's task was considerably lightened by the assistance of twelve readers, experts in the wide range of disciplines covered in the competition, who carefully screened the theses submitted. The Foundation joins the Committee in acknowledging their debt to Professors Paul E. Breer of Cornell University, Earl F. Cheit and Lyman W. Porter of the University of California at Berkeley, James R. Jackson of the University of California at Los Angeles, Arch R. Dooley of Harvard University, Daniel M. Holland of the Massachusetts Institute of Technology, Robert J. Holloway of the University of Minnesota, Donald P. Jacobs of Northwestern University, Bernard Karsh of the University of Illinois, Walter G. Kell of the University of Michigan, E. W. Martin, Jr. of Indiana University, and Joseph W. Newman of Stanford University.

With the publication of these latest winners, the Doctoral Dissertation Competition has completed its planned five-year span. My colleagues and I wish to express our appreciation for the generous assistance which the Ford Foundation has received from many people: Faculty members too numerous to mention have read and screened the more than 250 dissertations which have been submitted during the life of the competition, and Prentice-Hall has contributed its services to the publicizing and publishing of the selected dissertations.

> CLARENCE H. FAUST
> VICE PRESIDENT
> THE FORD FOUNDATION

New York, N.Y.
January, 1964

Acknowledgments

I acknowledge with gratitude the encouragement, advice, and criticism that my dissertation committee has given me. To Dean R. M. Cyert, Chairman, whose early interest encouraged me to undertake the project and whose continuing interest, both in the thesis and in my professional career, has been valued; to Professor A. H. Meltzer, whose insistence that I clarify and extend the argument in places that I had thought were entirely obvious has led to significant improvements in detail and perspective; to Professor H. A. Simon, from whose preceding research I have benefited greatly and whose critical views on methodology have helped me sharpen my own; to Professor L. A. Rapping, with whom I have enjoyed numerous stimulating discussions—often on topics that deal with the extension of the analysis to problems not explicitly included in the thesis.

In addition, I should also like to express my appreciation to Professor H. J. Leavitt for suggesting ways to improve parts of the argument; to Professor J. G. March, from whom I received my first exposure to organization theory and whose insights into the relations between economic theory and organizational analysis have stimulated my own; to Professor J. F. Muth for critical comments on an early version of the basic model; and to Dr. R. R. Nelson, for a series of discussions on the fruitfulness of applying conventional economic analysis to many of the issues raised by the "Carnegie School."

I should also like to thank my colleague, M. J. Hamburger, with whom I have exchanged views on a number of issues common to his research and mine, and the organizations that cooperated with me in developing the material reported in Chapter VI. Substantially all of the empirical results reported in Chapter VII, together with a brief statement of the model, appeared in the December 1963 issue of the *American Economic Review*. I am grateful for permission to include these materials here.

I have been fortunate to receive research support from the Ford Foundation both for a predoctoral fellowship under which the thesis was initiated and for a dissertation fellowship under which it was completed. In addition, summer research assistance from the Graduate

School of Industrial Administration, Carnegie Institute of Technology, has permitted me to advance the date of completion by several months.

Finally, I should like to acknowledge the exceptional moral support that I have received from my family. In particular, I should like to express my appreciation to my wife, Dolores, for her unfailing encouragement and assistance, and to my son, Scott, who, together with his sisters, displayed enormous patience. Indeed, with the thesis now completed while his schooling is about to begin, the ground rules under which the thesis has been written appear to be ones that he enthusiastically endorses—for he informs me that next year when he brings his brief case home from kindergarten, he will "go to the study, sit down at the desk, and tell the girls to be quiet."

OLIVER E. WILLIAMSON

Contents

CHAPTER 4

**A MORPHOLOGY OF MODELS OF THE BUSINESS FIRM:
I, MANAGERIAL DISCRETION MODELS**

APPENDIX 4A

**CORPORATION TAXES: INCOME AND SUBSTITUTION
EFFECTS**

APPENDIX 4B

THE SCOPE OF QUALITATIVE ECONOMICS EXTENDED

CHAPTER 5

**A MORPHOLOGY OF MODELS OF THE BUSINESS FIRM: II,
ENTREPRENEURIAL MODELS AND SALES MAXIMIZATION
HYPOTHESIS**

CHAPTER 6

THE EVIDENCE FROM THE FIELD STUDIES

CHAPTER 7

PRINCIPAL FIRM ANALYSIS   127

APPENDIX 7A

FIRMS AND INDUSTRIES INCLUDED IN THE ANALYSIS   140

APPENDIX 7B

SOURCES OF THE DATA   143

CHAPTER 8

SOCIAL CHOICE IN AN INSTITUTIONAL CONTEXT   145

CHAPTER 9

THE ECONOMICS
OF DISCRETIONARY BEHAVIOR:
MANAGERIAL OBJECTIVES
IN A THEORY OF THE FIRM

CHAPTER 1

Some Perspectives

The importance of managerial discretion in the operations of the large business firm has long been a troublesome question. To some observers it has been almost self-evident that the opportunities for discretion are extensive and that discretionary behavior is widely exhibited, while to others it has been unclear that in any significant sense such options even exist, much less are exercised. Progress in answering this question has been impaired by the frequent failure to combine descriptive with theoretical work and by the tendency, on both sides of the argument, to substitute anecdotal evidence for systematic empirical analysis.[1] Thus the occasional attempts to deal with this issue have usually been either expository, and have terminated short of an effort to integrate managerial objectives with the theory of the firm, or detached formalisms which possess broad generality but lack specific relevance for studying the effects of these objectives on business behavior. As a result, those who believe that discretionary behavior is important have tended to be imprecise in specifying how this influences the allocation of resources or the distribution of income, and this has permitted those who hold that such behavior is unimportant to treat deviations from the profit maximizing norm as negligible or to explain these away by *ad hoc* constructions.

If this condition is to be corrected, the following questions need to be answered: What are the primary motives of the management? Can these be provided with operational significance? If so, can such a translation of managerial objectives be introduced into a theory of the firm

---

[1] A notable exception is Gary S. Becker's, *The Economics of Discrimination* [12].

from which meaningful theorems can be derived? And if such an analytical framework can be provided, the question becomes: What is the evidence that discretion has a significant and systematic impact on business behavior? For example, how do differences in competition in the product market, in managerial tastes, and in the diffusion of stockholders influence the allocation of resources within the business firm? And how do regulatory or other profit constraints affect discretionary behavior?

Although these questions by no means exhaust the list of relevant issues, they constitute a beginning. In attempting to respond to these questions I have (1) drawn from the work of organization theorists in an attempt to discover the primary motives that influence managers, (2) used the conventional tools of economic analysis to develop the implications of a model constructed about these managerial objectives, and (3) combined field study and statistical techniques to study the effects of discretion on business behavior. Thus, whereas I retain the basic rationality assumption and deal with many of the same issues as the classical theory of the firm, I interpret the motivation for economic behavior somewhat more broadly than the classical theory and extend the range of issues upon which insights are obtained.

Within the domain of perfect competition (broadly conceived),[2] there is general agreement that the classical theory of the firm is an exceptionally parsimonious and accurate description of behavior. It is not always appreciated, however, that this theory achieves its power because of the constraints on the "opportunity set"[3] of choices that are open to the firm under these circumstances rather than because of the inherent accuracy of its behavioral assumptions. Where competitors are numerous and entry is easy, persistent departures from profit maximizing behavior inexorably lead to extinction. Economic natural selection holds the stage. In these circumstances, the behavior of the individual units that constitute the supply side of the product market is essentially routine and uninteresting and economists can confidently predict industry behavior without being explicitly concerned with the behavior of these individual units.

When the conditions of competition are relaxed, however, the opportunity set of the firm is expanded.[4] In this case, the behavior of the firm as a distinct operating unit is of separate interest. Both for purposes of

---

[2] For a broad interpretation of the requisite conditions of perfect competition, see Stigler [122, pp. 272–73].

[3] For an insightful exposition of the notion of "opportunity set," see Becker [13] [15].

[4] A general discussion of these effects is provided by Kaysen [69].

interpreting particular behavior within the firm as well as for predicting responses of the industry aggregate, it may be necessary to identify the factors that influence the firm's choices within this expanded opportunity set and embed these in a formal model. It is precisely with this latter group of firms that the present analysis is concerned.

1. Antecedents to the Analysis

Surely it is significant that the second and third chapters of Genesis record that where discretion exists it is apt to be exercised, and that merely to charge someone to be a good and faithful servant is not adequate to secure his performance. And clearly even a casual examination of the history of mankind reveals the substantial accuracy of these observations.

Yet, the assumption that the firm is operated in the stockholders best interests requires that, either voluntarily or of necessity, managers can be relied upon to behave in this ideal manner. Since the conditions of necessity are not ubiquitous, such an assumption obviously involves a contradiction with an impressive array of evidence. Indeed, there would appear to be little need to cite further grounds for developing a model of the firm that replaces unfailing stewardship behavior with a degree of self-interest seeking. Still, there is a certain degree of confidence that one can obtain for his views only by establishing precedence for them from within his profession. Consider therefore the following antecedents to this position.

1.1. Early Expressions of Support. The belief that managerial discretion has an important influence on the resource allocation process within the business firm has a long and recurrent history among economists. Support for this view can be traced to Adam Smith who found in monopoly the opportunity for managers to operate the firm to their advantage. Thus he observed that a grant of perpetual monopoly "is merely to enable the company to support the negligence, profusion, and malversation of their own servants, whose disorderly conduct seldom allows the company to exceed the ordinary rate of profit in trades which are altogether free" [117, p. 712]. Although this is a stronger statement of the effects of discretion than the one I shall propose, quite clearly it favors the construction of a theory that takes the individual self-interest seeking of those in effective control of the organization into account and gives little comfort to approaches that suppress these considerations.

Similarly, none other than the principal architect and master builder of the theory of perfect competition, Alfred Marshall, recognized that the operations of the joint stock company might well depart from the entrepreneurial model. Had Marshall's work terminated with the *Principles* there would be little in what he has to say that would support the position that I am advocating here.[5] The *Principles*, however, were followed by his *Industry and Trade*, and from his preface it is clear that he regards these two as, in some sense, companion volumes [84, p. vi]. Whereas the *Principles* were concerned with providing a statement of the fundamentals of economic theory, *Industry and Trade* had as its objective the "study of industrial technique and business organization." In it he evidences a more immediate concern with actual operations in the firm.

Marshall observes that the separation of ownership from control in the typical joint stock company makes effective criticism of management for anything less than gross negligence unlikely. Profit objectives, in these circumstances, may be subordinated [84, pp. 317–18], and where this occurs expansion of operations will tend to be favored. Indeed, this may proceed quite uncritically:

> There is one direction in which the extension of its operations by a great company, or by a department of municipal administration, is a source of danger that may be overlooked: It is that routine work by departments of a large business may expand at the expense of small businesses with greater elasticity and power of origination. The growth of a sense of moral responsibility among the chief technical employees of large concerns may be a partial remedy for this danger: But they cannot always approach a proposal for enlarging an existing department, or starting a new one, without some bias....
>
> There is a move upwards, and an increase of salaries all along the line, and everyone is pleased. So the movement grows; while a true balance of its advantages and disadvantages is perhaps never made out [84, pp. 321–22].

---

[5] See, however, his views on pages 302–4 and 604 in [83]. Although Marshall acknowledged a tendency for the firm to depart from the profit maximization model (due to the self-interest seeking behavior of its employees), he also observed that "anyone who is worth anything carries his higher nature with him into business; and, there as elsewhere, he is influenced by his personal affections, by his conceptions of duty and his reverence for high ideals" [83, p. 14]. With this I completely agree, and where such attitudes are present in large measure, and where the conceptions of duty are primarily to the stockholders, deviations from profit maximizing behavior are possibly negligible.

It would seem that to rely entirely on the competitive model as the engine of analysis for the study of all firms in all circumstances was not Marshall's intent. And despite the fact that he did not provide a formal model responsive to his observations, presumably they possess relevance for one who would attempt such a reconstruction.

Berle and Means examined the effects of the separation of ownership from control in more detail in their classic study, *The Modern Corporation and Private Property*. They took the position that where the separation of ownership and control is substantial, "control may be held by the directors or titular managers who can employ the proxy machinery to become a self-perpetuating body, even though as a group they own but a small fraction of the stock outstanding" [18, p. 5].

After examining the extent to which economic power is concentrated in large corporations, the degree of dispersion of stock ownership, and the distribution of effective control, Berle and Means posed the crucial question of possible differences in the interests between the management and the stockholders. Thus they inquired,

> ... have we any justification for assuming that those in control of a modern corporation will also choose to operate it in the interests of the stockholders? The answer to this question will depend on the degree to which the self-interest of those in control may run parallel to the interests of ownership and, insofar as they differ, on the checks on the use of power which may be established by political, economic, or social conditions [18, p. 121].

Others who have expressed views at variance with the profit maximization assumption include J. M. Keynes, who observed that when stockholders are "almost entirely dissociated from the management, ... the direct personal interest of the latter in making a profit becomes quite secondary" [71, p. 316]. And J. R. Hicks, in his 1935 survey of monopoly theory, suggested that the "quiet life," rather than pecuniary gain, was "the best of all monopoly profits" [63, p. 8]. Although to assign profit to a secondary position and the quiet life to primacy is somewhat extreme, it should be clear that one who is not altogether content with the profit maximization assumption has distinguished antecedents. Indeed, within the last 15 years, discontent with the profit maximization assumption has been widely expressed.

1.2. Contemporary Expression of Support. Recent dissatisfaction with the profit maximization assumption has been one of two types. Either it is claimed that maximization is a nonoperational concept and hence a different analytical framework is required, or the exclusive attention to the profit goal is disputed. The "marginalist controversy" of the late 1940's was concerned with the first of these objections,[6] but it neglected the issue of providing a useful substitute. It was thus a somewhat barren methodological discussion. Simon has since emphasized the importance of replacing maximizing by adaptive behavior [112] and the Cyert and March "behavioral" approach to the theory of the firm is precisely concerned with constructing a model responsive to this objective [38].

With the exception of some of my remarks in Chapter 9, my analysis neglects this type of objection and focuses instead on the motivational assumptions. Those who have disputed (often for different reasons), the efficacy of restricting the motivation for economic behavior in the business firm to profits include Gordon [54], Hurwicz [66], Reder [95], Cooper [35], Papandreou [92], Graaff [55], Bowen [22], Simon [110], Baumol [11], Kaysen [69], Becker [12] [13] [14], and Alchian and Kessel [2]. Support for the proposition that discretion may have an important influence on the allocation of resources within the firm has also been expressed by Stigler [123, p. 35] and Scitovsky [104, pp. 106–8]. Since many of these positions will be reviewed in Chapter 2, no restatement will be given here.

2. Preliminary Statement of the Basic Approach

My analysis centers attention on the discretionary behavior of managers in their operation of the business firm. With the exception of some of the remarks in the concluding chapter, the viewpoint is neutral: neither approval nor disapproval of these discretionary activities is intended. Rather, my objective is merely (1) to indicate in what respects managers may be motivated to attend to other-than-profit goals, (2) to translate the motivation of managers to an analysis of operations context, (3) to identify the necessary conditions for discretionary behavior to be of quantitative importance, (4) to develop the implications, direct and indirect, of a theory based on this position, and (5) to examine the evidence of such behavior.

For these purposes the relationship of organization theory to the theory of the firm is of special importance. Organization theory takes more of a systems approach than is characteristic of psychology and is

---

[6] For reference to and an evaluation of this controversy, see Friedman [50, pp. 15–16].

more concerned with the pertinent subset of behavior, from the stand-point of the theory of the firm, than sociology. Furthermore, it serves to integrate the contributions of both of these disciplines. Thus, for purposes of relating the other social sciences to economics so as to discover organizational phenomena that have important economic conse-quences (but with which economists may have little experience), organ-ization theory provides a particularly appropriate bridge. Indeed, that economists have not been more successful in building models that have organizationally interesting properties must be partly attributed to their neglect of the contributions that organization theorists have made.

The reason for such neglect is largely due to the limited interest economists have had in the theory of the firm. Aggregate or market behavior has usually been the chief object of their analyses and the behavior of individual firms, or components of those firms, has been subordinated to this objective. Thus, theories of the firm with convenient aggregation properties have been given preference to those which, by emphasizing relevancy at the level of the individual firm, complicated the problem of aggregation.

As Samuelson [100] and Simon [115] have recently reminded us, however, it is possible that this emphasis on convenience in aggregation has tended to oversimplify or obscure problems of importance in the monopolistic sector. Here, a theory of the firm more specifically con-cerned with the characteristics of that sector may be required if we are to deal effectively with nontrivial problems of discretionary behavior. Whether the gains from simplicity in the structure of the analysis justify the costs can only be determined by examining the results obtainable from alternative constructions.

If economists are to respond to this challenge and specifically inquire into the processes by which firms are operated, obviously there is a need for fundamental organizational insights. For such a purpose, organization theory can play a vital role. Its emphasis on basic group processes, on positive rather than normative behavior, and on providing a structure for interpreting this behavior makes it a fertile source for the discovery of the critical behavioral assumptions needed by the economist in his attempt at a reconstruction.

For the present analysis, organization theory both suggested which kinds of phenomena were relevant for the understanding of organizational behavior and provided a connected framework with which to interpret them. Consider the following propositions: behavior is responsive to perceived rather than hypothetical rewards; personal goals influence organizational participation; organizational slack is absorbed by knowledgeable and active participants; organizational viability requires a value consensus and hence precludes arbitrary assignment of goals; individuals achieve an economy of effort by selective pursuit of goals in accordance with the capacity of the environment to produce satisfaction.[7] Taken separately each of these is suggestive of interesting hypotheses concerning organizational behavior. Collectively, however, and particularly if digested into a formal model, they produce much more powerful insights.

3. Organization of the Analysis

Chapter 2, like this one, is concerned with developing perspectives. It reviews some of the recent arguments for revising the theory of the firm, examines intended a priori grounds for preferring the profit maximization assumption, and indicates in what respects my analysis is responsive to the revisionist literature.

The motivational foundation for the proposed model is developed in Chapter 3. This is regarded as an essential part of the analysis. It is intended not merely as a basis for formal model construction, but also for the value it possesses in devising tests of particular behavior.

The basic "managerial discretion" models are provided in Chapter 4. Equilibrium and comparative statics properties are developed and, in a casual sense, related to behavior. Chapter 5 continues the formal model building and attention is successively directed to the usual (or short-run) profit maximizing model, the discounted (or long-run) profit maximizing model, and the sales maximization hypothesis of Baumol's [11]. Similarities and differences with the managerial discretion models are discussed.

The next two chapters are concerned with a survey of the evidence. Chapter 6 examines the evidence from a group of field studies and suggests that the processes observed, as well as the magnitudes of the responses that occurred, are generally consistent with the managerial discretion model. Tests of particular behavior are given in Chapter 7. The results again support the proposition that discretionary opportunities have a significant influence on business behavior.

Since the managerial discretion model substitutes a general preference function for single-component functions, the issue of social choice is

---

[7] The first of these propositions can be found in March and Simon [81, pp. 51, 62], the second in March and Simon [81, p. 65] and Thompson [126, p. 81], the third in Cyert and March [38, Chap. 3], the fourth in a number of sociological references, e.g., Fallding [46, p. 10], and the last was first suggested to me by Professor March in conversation.

bound to arise. Chapter 8 is concerned with the question of organizational viability. The need for a substantial value consensus is examined, the process for obtaining one is described, and the effects of consensus are developed. Under a set of circumstances more general than those required of the usual theories of the firm, the proposed model is shown to return consistent results.

The principal findings are summarized in Chapter 9, and a brief statement of the relevance of the analysis for economic policy is provided. I conclude with a statement of directions for future research.

CHAPTER 2

Revisions to the Theory of the Firm

Research on the theory of the firm can be conveniently separated into two groups: normative prescriptions for improving the operations of the firm, and positive analyses describing the operations of the firm. The management science literature is characteristic of the first group. Since reviews of the recent contributions of this group are available elsewhere[1] and since this literature is not essential to the issues that are of concern here, I will proceed directly to an examination of several of the recent studies that have been concerned with the positive aspects of business behavior. Following this, possible a priori bases for establishing the superiority of the profit maximization assumption are examined.

1. Positive Contributions to the Theory of the Firm

Positive studies in the theory of the firm have generally proceeded in either of two directions. Although they are not mutually exclusive, both have rarely been pursued simultaneously. One has emphasized realism in process (with some casual references to the issue of motivation), while the other has emphasized realism in motivational assumptions (with some indirect implications for the understanding of process). Although my chief interest here is in the second of these, a brief review

---

[1] *Vide* [35] [41] [114].

of the "realism-in-process" approach will be useful for purposes of perspective.

1.1. Realism in Process. These studies argue that concepts like profit maximization are nonoperational and that a more relevant theory would be one that examines the types of information processing that actually occur in the firm and are important to business decisions. By studying real rather than hypothetical stimuli, a more fundamental theory of business behavior would, it is believed, result.

Boulding and Cooper have voiced common but separate beliefs that a reorientation based on balance sheet considerations would place economists in touch with the type of data that influence businessmen [21] [34]. A more realistic theory of the firm, it is claimed, would result: one which would not only permit the economists to predict firm behavior better than the classical theory but, indeed, one which would be of genuine assistance to the executive in planning his operations. Despite the persuasive manner in which these proposals have been advanced, models that achieve these results have not been forthcoming.

A more recent and more successful approach to the realism-in-process objective has been the "behavioral" theory of the firm work of Cyert and March [38]. They have chosen the decision process as the critical unit for analysis. Where decision making is characterized by intended, but bounded, rationality, adaptive rather than maximizing processes will characterize the behavior of the firm. Their objective is to examine the implications of this position for the internal allocation of resources in the business firm.

Although much of what they have to say has relevance for the present analysis—in particular their use of the notion of "organization slack" [38, pp. 36–38]—they tend not to treat the motivation question directly. Instead, they permit motivation to manifest itself through behavior. Thus, although motivational considerations are present, they enter less directly than in studies explicitly concerned with the "realism-in-motivation" problem.

1.2. Realism in Motivation. This approach emphasizes the possible effects on behavior of the opportunities for discretion in the operations of the business firm. Where the range of behavior that is consistent with survival is narrowly bounded, the question of motivation is of small importance. However, some firms appear to have access to advantages that bring substantial relief from the threat of extinction. Here an understanding of motivation may be essential.

1.2.1. Gordon: A Study of Business Leadership. Of principal interest in Gordon's 1945 study of business leadership [54] were his observations that (1) the power and discretion of the management in the typical large corporation vastly exceeds that imputed to it by classical theory and (2) rather than acting solely in a stewardship role of protecting the stockholders interests, the management (as is entirely natural) also considers interests of its own. Allowance for the effects of these non-pecuniary motives is, in his view, essential to an understanding of business behavior [54, pp. 305–16]. Since subsequent work on the theory of the firm has largely failed to reflect these considerations, Gordon was led to observe in the preface to the recent edition that "we still need a theory of the firm that takes account of [organizational] factors" [54, p. xiv]. More specifically he suggests that

> The development of the large corporation has obviously affected the goals of business decision-making . . . . Almost certainly the personal and group goals of higher and lower executives are a part of the total value system—the desires for security, power, prestige, advancement within the organization, and so on. One result, almost certainly, is that the maintenance of satisfactory profits is a more accurate statement of the profits objective than is complete profits-maximization. Perhaps it is not inaccurate to say that *profits are viewed as the basic constraint subject to which other goals can be followed.* Subject to this constraint, some profits will be sacrified in pursuit of other goals [54, p. xii]. (Italics added.)

Although there are other factors associated with current business practices (including the trend towards scientific management[2]) that Gordon would like to see included in a theory of the firm, I shall be content in this analysis to try to answer to the description above.

1.2.2. Papandreou: A Survey. Papandreou's declared purpose in his 1952 survey article was to demonstrate that organization theory provided the economist with the necessary concepts for performing a useful reconstruction of the theory of the firm. The objective was an ambitious one and perhaps not entirely realized.[3] Nonetheless his remarks stand as an

---

[2] The view that "scientific management" tends to cause the firm to be operated more nearly as a profit maximizer has been widely expressed but rarely precisely. Is it responsible for additional constraints on the management, or only for greater productivity per unit of input?

[3] For confirmation of this position, see Simon [113, p. xxix, n. 8].

important bridge between the classical theory of the firm and subsequent efforts at revision.

As the remarks in the previous chapter indicated, the value of organization theory to economists is less in the formal connections that can be established between the two than in the behavioral insights that organization theory can provide to economists. Papandreou's analysis represents an effort to merge these insights with certain of the revisionist observations of Gordon [54], Berle and Means [18], Schumpeter [102], and other economists who alleged that economic theory had failed to deal effectively with a broad class of phenomena that are of general importance for the understanding of business behavior. Among his observations that are of particular interest to the present analysis are the following:

1. Stockholders are seldom in a position to exercise decisive control in the typical large firm. Their demands, more often, take the form of a minimum performance constraint [92, pp. 197–98].
2. "Rationality is consistent with the maximization of other things as well as profits. Profit maximization can be derived from utility-index maximization only through the imposition of a restriction on the character of the index" [92, p. 206].
3. "We should proceed to substitute general preference-function maximation for profit maximization .... [However], it is much harder to derive operationally meaningful theorems concerning firm behavior from a construction which is directly based on preference-function maximization than to do so from the profit maximization construction. The relative development of the theory of the firm (based on profit maximization) as contrasted to that of the consumer (based on utility-index maximization) testifies to the validity of the argument" [92, p. 211].
4. The entrepreneur should be replaced by a "peak coordinator" whose function is to successfully reconcile the internal (mainly managerial) and external influences that impinge on the firm so as to maintain a viable organization [92, p. 193]. Such a formulation, however, should not be used merely as a device for dodging the social choice issue. Explicit concern with this problem may be essential [92, pp. 211–12].

Points 1 and 2 are examined in more detail later in this chapter and the next. The suggestion (in point 3) that a general preference function be formulated is adopted in the models proposed in Chapter 4. Fortunately, however, his belief that the derivation of operationally meaningful theorems is thereby made much more difficult is not entirely correct. The social choice issue that he raises in point 4 occupies our attention in Chapter 8. By emphasizing the internal influences that promote consensus and by having only loose regard for external influences, a variant on his "peak coordinator" suggestion is shown to have general relevance.

1.2.3. Bowen: Research on Business Behavior. Bowen, assisted by a select committee of social scientists, prepared an overall study of the need for research on the business firm for the Social Sciences Research Council [22]. He regards research on the firm as an interdisciplinary matter and suggests that the lack of integration of social psychology and sociology with economics has been responsible for many of the failures to deal effectively with internal problems of motivation and control.

His framework for revision to the theory of the firm follows Papandreou in many respects, but he extends it to include a wide variety of specific business activities which, in his opinion, deserve detailed attention. Indeed, like Simon, he argues that an understanding of internal operations is necessary to the prediction of overt behavior. Not only should the processes of business decision making be studied, but the very motivational foundations of a theory of the firm require re-examination: does the accumulating evidence really support the economists' assumption of profit maximization?

In addition to his pleas for interdisciplinary cooperation in the study of the business firm, Bowen suggests that empirical rather than theoretical studies should receive primary emphasis. These empirical studies should be directed toward gaining an understanding of specific, detailed aspects of business behavior.

Although Bowen's emphasis on interdisciplinary research, the study of particular behavior in the business firm, and the importance of re-examining motivational foundations are generally unobjectionable, it is not clear that empirical studies should precede rather than follow new theoretical constructions. The approach followed here has been first to discover what agreement existed on managerial motivation, next to introduce appropriate motivational assumptions into a formal model, and finally to examine the evidence in the context of this theoretical framework. The advantages of such a sequence should be obvious.

1.2.4. Simon: A Persistent Advocate of Revision. There is perhaps no more persistent contemporary advocate of moving the theory of the firm in the direction of greater realism than Simon. His objections to the classical theory turn on two important differences between "economic" and "social" man. The difference most often stressed by Simon is that the former is a maximizing while the latter is an adaptive organism [109] [110, p. 166] [112]. It is his contention that "to predict the short-run behavior of an adaptive organism, or its behavior in a complex and rapidly changing environment, it is not enough to know its goals. We must know also a great deal about its internal structure and particularly its mechanisms of adaptation" [112, p. 255].

The second difference Simon emphasizes is that economic man obtains none of his satisfactions within the organization. "In accepting employment, the employee turns off the switch of his own desires from nine to five and *accepts criteria unrelated to his own personal goals as the basis for his decisions and behavior*" [110, p. 167]. (Italics added.) If this is not substantially true but instead the employees, more particularly the managers, do receive satisfactions within the firm and therefore are influenced by the prospects of internal rewards, a modification in the theory of the firm that takes this into account may be useful.

Ideally, attempts at revision would reflect both parts of this double-barreled criticism of the classical theory. However, it is often easier to proceed piecewise. Thus, with the exception of some of the remarks in Chapter 9, the present analysis neglects the first of these objections and focuses entirely on the second.

1.2.5. Kaysen: The Effects of Discretion. Kaysen is concerned with the impact of the large corporation over a wide range of economic, political, and social conditions. He finds that a large segment of manufacturing industry and most of the regulated sector of the economy (utilities, transportation, finance) are characterized by large absolute size and suggests that this size, together with barriers to entry of various sorts, effectively insulates these firms from the compulsions of competition and opens up a wide range of discretionary choice to their managements [69, p. 89]. As long as these firms earn an "acceptable" return, the option of pursuing any of a number of nonprofit objectives is available to them [69, pp. 90–91].

Discretion to the firm and to the management is treated interchangeably since "corporate management is typically—in the reaches of business we are examining—an autonomous center of decision, organizing the affairs of the corporation and choosing its own successors" [69, p. 91]. Stockholders are not entirely neglected, but their objectives are only one of a number of competing influences that the management attends to in directing the affairs of the firm [69, p. 91].

Kaysen identifies four economic areas in which the effects of the large firm require scrutiny: economic efficiency, industrial stability, technical progress, and equity. In examining their performance in each of these he finds that, with respect to efficiency, stability, and equity, the discretion associated with size produces generally unfavorable results, while the verdict is at best mixed on the issue of technical progress [69, pp. 92–99]. The remainder of his analysis takes us beyond the range of the present study and is concerned with the political and social effects of the large corporation on American culture. On these issues, his judgment is almost wholly unfavorable [69, pp. 100–3].

Size as such is less of an issue in the present analysis than is the extent to which size is combined with the absence of competition. Since the correlation between these two is probably substantial (indeed, Edwards finds "conglomerate bigness" to be a separate source of monopoly power [44]), this qualification may frequently be unnecessary. To neglect it, however, may be the source of some confusion.

In examining the effects of discretion on business behavior, the present study makes use of the acceptable return hypothesis, and the terms "management" and "firm" are frequently used interchangeably. Of the four areas for analysis that Kaysen suggests, emphasis is placed on the way in which the discretionary allocation of resources affects economic efficiency, stability, and equity, while the technical progress issue is neglected.

1.2.6. Becker: Effects of Monopoly on Discrimination. Becker characterizes his study of the economics of race and religious discrimination as one with general relevance and application. Thus, he observes,

> This theory is applicable not only to discrimination and nepotism in the market place but also to non-market discrimination and nepotism and, indeed, more generally to other kinds of non-pecuniary motivation as well. From this viewpoint the major contribution of the book is to develop a theory of non-pecuniary motivation and to apply it quantitatively to discrimination in the market place. It is my belief that this application will stimulate the quantitative analysis of non-pecuniary motivation in other areas [12, p. 3].

The economic model that he develops for studying the effects of discrimination is both general and ingenious. It is not obvious, however, how to extend it to include the sorts of considerations that are of concern here. Thus, while his analysis and statistical results provide support for the proposition that managerial "tastes" and the opportunity for discretion have an important influence on the operations of the business firm, it has been more convenient to construct a separate model than to attempt to apply his.

1.2.7. Alchian and Kessel: Regulated Monopoly and Nonpecuniary Goals. Although their analysis is conducted entirely at a verbal level and they confine their attention to the operations of regulated firms, the description of behavior provided by Alchian and Kessel parallels mine in a number of respects. Their basic proposal, like mine, is that a utility function that includes personal goals be substituted for the profit maximization assumption [2, p. 158]. They examine the implications of this position for the operations of public utilities and firms subject to potential antitrust prosecution and observe that the cardinal sin of these firms is to be too profitable or to acquire too large a market share. Such firms are thus induced to consciously absorb profits by attending to nonpecuniary objectives.

It is curious, however, that Alchian and Kessel find no reason for large size, the diffusion of ownership, or (presumably) high concentration in the product market to produce these same effects in the nonregulated sector of the economy [2, pp. 165–66]. As is argued below, the operations of the capital market, which they apparently find to effectively eliminate discretionary activities in the nonregulated sector [2, p. 160], may actually be an ineffectual constraint within a broad range. Thus public utilities are treated as a *special case* of the general model of nonregulated, discretionary behavior that is proposed.

2. Profit Maximization Reconsidered

That models responsive to the preceding considerations have not been more common is undoubtedly due to the general belief that there are substantial a priori grounds for preferring the profit maximization assumption. Partly, but certainly not entirely, this may be due to the prevalence of the perfectly competitive model in the work of economists.

The assumption of profit maximization followed from the assumption of perfect competition as a necessary consequence. And even where the assumptions of perfect competition are only approximately fulfilled (as, of course, is all that is possible),[4] the use of the profit maximization assumption as a survival condition is justified. However, once one departs from the large numbers case, its great a priori plausibility is no longer secure.[5] Instead, application of this assumption to situations that explicitly assume a degree of monopoly would seem to require separate justification. It is the objective of this section to show that logical arguments for demonstrating the superiority of the profit maximization assumption generally imply conditions concerning the state of the world of an empirical rather than a logical variety.

2.1. Rational Behavior and Profit Maximization. Using a model that permitted the entrepreneur to choose only between work and leisure, Scitovsky has ingeniously shown that the entrepreneur who was maximizing his utility would simultaneously maximize his profit only if his indifference curves between income and leisure were vertical displacements of one another [103, p. 356]. This requires that, given the level of activity (or of leisure), the marginal rate of substitution of income for leisure be the same at every level of income.[6] In other words, "the entrepreneur's choice between more or less activity—or between more income and more leisure—must be independent of his income" [103, p. 356].

Scitovsky suggests that the requisite psychology to assure such a result prevailed in the early days of capitalism—where "the combination

---

[4] For example, the assumption of perfect foresight in the model is never satisfied. However, all that is required in order for the main implications of the model to obtain is that the accumulation of information with respect to cost and demand conditions be used constructively by the *large* number of firms, extant and potential, that constitute the industry. See Stigler [122, pp. 272–73].

[5] As Reder has observed, it is not always appreciated that it was the anterior assumption of perfect competition that provided the profit maximization assumption its a priori plausibility [95, p. 454].

[6] That this is so can be seen as follows: Let $U = U(\pi, L)$, where U = utility, π = income, and L = leisure. Then $dU = \dfrac{\partial U}{\partial \pi} d\pi + \dfrac{\partial U}{\partial L} dL$. Since along an indifference curve $dU = 0$, the marginal rate of substitution is given by: MRS = $-\dfrac{d\pi}{dL} = \dfrac{\partial U/\partial L}{\partial U/\partial \pi}$. What is required for the vertical displacement condition to be satisfied is that, given the level of activity (leisure), $d\pi/dL$ be independent of income, i.e., a constant. But if $\dfrac{d\pi}{dL}\bigg|_L$ is constant, then, from the expression above, it is seen that the marginal rate of substitution of income for leisure, given the level of leisure, must be constant.

of frugality and industry ... [was] calculated to insure the independence of the entrepreneur's willingness to work from the level of income"—and may be approximately true today [103, pp. 357–58]. If correct, this means that profit can be properly substituted for utility, and models that employ profit maximization reflect rational choice at a more general level than might at first be apparent.

Debating the intuitive appeal of a constant marginal rate of substitution of income for leisure (given the level of leisure) is hardly apt to prove fruitful. Fundamentally, this is an empirical question and can scarcely be resolved at a purely conjectural level.[7] The justification for the profit maximization assumption is its usefulness [103, p. 60], and whereas this may be substantial for some purposes, it may be less valuable for others. It is one of the objectives of the present analysis to help determine more exactly these bounds of usefulness.

A second variety of argument intended to establish the identity of utility with profit is that "since firms constitute the intermediate not the final sector of the economy, and ... since money is in our society the universal means for accomplishing any ends whatsoever, profit maximization is fully consistent [with] the maximization of utility indexes in the final or consumer sector of the economy."[8] If true, of course, this would end the discussion. But it assumes that *private* personal consumption is the sole intent of all economic activity in the firm. It ignores that the allocation of resources within the firm by those who control the decision-making machinery can be done in ways that selectively promote the decision makers' interests at the possible expense of profit. To develop this point here would anticipate the argument of the following chapters. Suffice it to point out that the "final sector" argument fails to establish this identity of utility and profit as long as the possibility of such anti-profit activity exists.

2.2. Economic Natural Selection.
The classic statement of the economic natural selection argument has been given by Alchian [1].

---

[7] Under ideal conditions, at least, the relation is potentially testable. Thus it requires that if the entrepreneur were awarded a lump-sum bounty or subjected to a lump-sum tax, that his allocation of energy be entirely unaffected. This is potentially testable by observing the behavior of entrepreneurs who have received windfall gains or losses. The condition also requires that the entrepreneur reduce his hours of work in response to an increase in the profits tax rate. This is also an observable.

[8] The argument is from Papandreou [91, p. 722]. It is not one that he endorses, but rather he identifies this as representing the position of those who insist on restricting the firm's preference function to profits.

The most compact summary of this position, however, is probably
Friedman's. The argument runs,

> Unless the behavior of businessmen in some way or other
> approximated behavior consistent with the maximization of
> returns, it seems unlikely that they would remain in business
> for long. Let the apparent immediate determinant of business
> behavior be anything at all—habitual reaction, random chance,
> or whatnot. Whenever this determinant happens to lead to
> behavior consistent with rational and informed maximization
> of returns, the business will prosper and acquire resources with
> which to expand; whenever it does not, the business will tend
> to lose resources and can be kept in existence only by the addi-
> tion of resources from outside. The process of "natural selec-
> tion" thus helps to validate the [maximization of net returns]
> hypothesis—or, rather, given natural selection, acceptance of
> the hypothesis can be based largely on the judgment that it
> summarizes appropriately the conditions for survival [50, p. 22].

That economic natural selection fails to provide a wholly satisfactory
basis for unqualified acceptance of the profit maximization hypothesis
has been argued by Koopmans. He takes the position that if economic
natural selection is the basis for our confidence in the profit maximization hypothesis,

> ... then we should postulate that basis itself and not the profit
> maximization which it implies in certain circumstances. We
> should then postulate that entrepreneurial policies unsuitable
> for economic survival are applied by only a minority of enter-
> prises which exhibit a high rate of economic mortality.
>
> Such a change in the basis of economic analysis would seem
> to represent a gain in realism attributable to a concern with
> directly perceived descriptive accuracy of the postulates. *It
> would lead us to expect profit maximization to be most clearly
> exhibited in industries where entry is easiest and where the struggle
> for survival is keenest,* and would present us with the further
> challenge to analyze what circumstances give to an industry
> that character [74, pp. 140–41]. (Italics added.)

In short, Koopmans recognizes that the conditions under which
economic natural selection implies profit maximization are not ubiquitous
and that where the conditions of competition are weak, models that
include other than profit goals may be appropriate. This is a vital point,

certainly critical to the present analysis and presumably important to economics generally. Recognition that economic natural selection is not wholly efficacious over the entire range of competitive conditions reveals that still another type of intended a priori argument for preferring the profit maximization assumption must be qualified to include a statement of the conditions of competition to which it applies.

It is significant that Winter, in his systematic examination of the natural selection argument, came to a similar conclusion [129]. He demonstrated that there were a number of critical assumptions (including "proposal" of the optimum strategy, "persistence" on these dimensions, a mechanism for "selection" on each of the dimensions, and "appropriate variation in the environment") and that the argument requires clarification with respect to each of these before it can be properly invoked. Indeed, he concludes his analysis with the observation that "there would seem to be a need in economics for more direct observation of business behavior and, of even greater importance, more adequate theory for summarizing the results of that observation in the cases where the profit maximization explanation is inadequate or cannot be made operational" [131, p. 75].

2.3. Competition in the Capital Market. Economic natural selection as an all-purpose argument appears to be suspect because it depends on a variety of competition in the product market that is not everywhere satisfied. An alternative approach for achieving a priori status for the profit maximization assumption is the competition in the capital market argument. Alchian and Kessel have stated it as follows:[9]

> Both the competitive and monopoly model imply that the assets of an enterprise, be it a monopolist or competitive firm, will be utilized by those for whom these assets have the greatest economic value. One might object to this implication of similarity between competition and monopoly by arguing that, when a monopolistic enterprise is not making the most of its pecuniary economic opportunities, it runs less risk of being driven out of business than a similarly mismanaged competitive enterprise. The answer to this is that despite the absence of competition in product markets, those who can most profitably utilize monopoly powers will acquire control over them: competition in the capital markets will allocate monopoly rights to those

---

[9] A similar statement appears in Becker [12, p. 38].

who can use them most profitably. Therefore, so long as free capital markets are available, the absence of competition in product markets does not imply a different quality of management in monopolistic as compared with competitive enterprises. Only in the case of nontransferable assets (human monopoly rights and powers like those commanded by Bing Crosby) does classical theory, given free capital market arrangements, admit a difference between competition and monopoly with respect to the effectiveness with which these enterprises pursue profits [2, p. 160].

As with the economic natural selection argument, the competition in the capital market position is incomplete. In order to operate as described, it requires that a *mechanism* exist whereby control over monopoly power can actually, and not just hypothetically, be transferred through the capital market. It requires that control over monopoly power reside with the stockholders rather than the managers and that this control be transferable through financial (capital market) rather than political (managerial ascension) processes.

As Berle and Means indicated [18], however, and as has been observed repeatedly since,[10] the stockholders may frequently exercise only a limited influence over the operations of the firm. This is particularly true when the stockholders are small and the ownership is dispersed [54, pp. 156-61]. But it is also true that actual or potential ownership by institutional investors, speculators, raiders, or large private stockholders may fail to transform the capital market into the efficacious exchange of monopoly power place suggested by the quotation above [97, pp. 53-54].

Although the influence of institutional investors is potentially great, this power has largely gone unexercised. As Gordon has observed,

> ... the managers of these funds carefully avoid interfering actively in the affairs of the companies whose stocks they own. Indeed, it seems to be generally true that these institutional investors automatically follow and support with their proxies the managements of the companies in whose stock they have invested .... Control in any active and meaningful sense is not associated with this sort of institutional ownership [54, p. vii].

---

[10] Mason, for example, takes the position that "almost everyone now agrees that in the large corporation the owner is, in general, a passive recipient; that typically control is in the hands of management; and that management normally selects its own replacements" [86, p. 4]. See also [54, pp. vi–x] and [97].

Speculators excel in trading securities, not in managing companies. Thus they are concerned with undervaluation *given* the existing management rather than undervaluation *due* to the existing management. Although they pay a great deal of attention to the condition of a company's stock, their interest is confined to trading opportunities. And although speculation in the company's securities may draw attention to internal conditions in the firm, it is apt to be restricted to financial conditions (for example, the liquidity position of the firm), and operating decisions and objectives are likely to be affected only tangentially. Hence, if an active influence over the affairs of the firm is to come from the capital market, it must derive largely from other sources.

It is sometimes believed that raiders constitute an important threat to existing managements and thereby place a genuine bound on the discretionary resource allocation processes within the firm. No doubt they have an effect. The real question is: How severe is the constraint that they impose? In general, as long as the firm earns modest profits, it seems unlikely that the raiders will be highly successful in generating the interest and support they usually require from other stockholders. For one thing, they have to contend with a proxy machinery that favors the incumbents. For another, the suspicion with which the average stockholder regards the motives of the raider typically prevents attempts at overturning the company executives unless the performance of the organization is clearly unacceptable.[11] Finally, even in those cases where the raiders have been successful in their efforts to gain control, their management of the enterprise has often failed to meet expectations.[12] For each of these reasons, the potential threat of raiders would appear to have only a moderate influence on the operations of the business firm.

The last group to consider is the large stockholder. This class can be split further into two types: large participant stockholders and large nonparticipant stockholders. Members of the management group who have large shareholdings in the firm constitute the first group. Those in the second group are not part of the management.

---

[11] As Knauth put it, "the degree of success that management must produce to remain in office is surprisingly small. Indeed management must fail obviously and even ignominiously before the dispersed forces of criticism become mobilized for action" [7, p. 45].

[12] Recent examples of raiders who have fallen substantially short of the mark as operators are Louis Wolfson [60] and the late Robert Young. Part of their difficulty may have been due to their dependence on a management substructure that had less than complete confidence in them and perceived the change at the top as a threat to its security. In such circumstances, dysfunctional behavior, with its attendant effects on performance, is likely to develop.

Before examining the influence of each of these two parties on the affairs of the firm, it may be well to indicate that by no means does every large firm have "large" stockholders of either type. Managers ordinarily own only a very small fraction of the shares outstanding in the typical large corporation [54, p. 27], and often they are not large shareholders absolutely. Similarly, individual holdings outside of the firm often do not account for any sizeable fraction of the total. Thus, in many firms, large stockholders of both types are simply nonexistent.

Where large stockholders of either type do exist, the direction of the effect they have on profit should be clear. The question of the magnitude of this effect, however, is less certain. Does the profit objective become effectively overriding, or is it merely enhanced?

Consider the case of the manager-stockholder first. As a manager he may be inclined to attend to certain nonprofit objectives. As a stockholder, profit is the main source of satisfaction. Combining these roles of manager and stockholder suggests that profit will be more highly valued than it would be in the role of manager alone, but not necessarily to the extinction of all other objectives. That is, a shift in the manager's preference function towards profit could be expected, but not necessarily domination by the profit component. Furthermore, since the firm's preference function is a composite of its most influential members (see Chapter 8), the preference of any individual manager-stockholder for profit will be moderated by the extent to which this preference is general.

Large stockholders outside of the corporation do not have the need to choose between alternative ways of obtaining their satisfactions. Greater profit is unambiguously in their interest. However, their lack of intimate contact with the firm's operating activities puts them at a relative disadvantage in any attempts to evaluate and influence operating decisions. At best they can lay down guidelines and evaluate gross performance. In this sense they can augment the attention to profit, but this is hardly to elevate profit to a position where it represents the firm's entire objective.

The possibility of merger presents an additional capital market influence to those considered above. The firm that is underachieving with respect to its profit potential may be favorably regarded as a candidate for merger by those firms that display a greater preference for profits. Thus a persistent tendency to replace nonprofit-maximizing managements by those with a greater profit orientation might possibly drive the former group out of existence. Before this displacement will be complete, however, it is first necessary that the firms with the higher profit preferences be fully knowledgeable of the unrealized profits available in other organizations. Where knowledge of the precise magnitude of the unrealized profits is imperfect, but estimates of the possible outcomes together with their associated probabilities are symmetrically distributed about the true value of the potential profits, risk aversion would tend to discourage mergers that would be attractive in the absence of uncertainty. If, in addition, imperfect knowledge generally leads to estimates of the possible outcomes that are biased downwards, merger interests will be all the less keen.

In addition to the information requirement, however, a further difficulty may block mergers between high and low profit preference managements. Bain designates this impediment as *enterprise sovereignty considerations*, by which we refer to the virtual deterrent to mergers inhering in the difficulty of potential participants in agreeing on terms, and fundamentally to the reluctance of individual ownership-management units to yield up their sovereign controls over their operations" [8, p. 184]. Taken together, these information and sovereignty considerations suggest that mergers are not likely to be the device by which low profit preference managements are fully displaced.

If these views are accepted, then we emerge with the result that, to the extent that stockholders are *knowledgeable, powerful,* and *active,* the capital market may indeed impose a moderately severe constraint on the behavior of the firm (and this may generalize to other firms through contacts in the product market). But since this triplet appears frequently to go unfulfilled, competition in the capital markets may fail to produce the intended effects. The proposed alternative to complete stockholder control over monopoly power is that a nontrivial fraction of this control is in the possession of the firm's management. The mechanism for transferring this latter type of monopoly power is a process of executive ascension and retirement. Thus, this power is exchanged through a political rather than a financial process and is not marketable in any usual sense.

Assuming that monopoly power is generally exercised to the advantage of those who possess it leads to the following hypothesis: classes of expenditures for which the management has a positive preference should be systematically related to the conditions of competition in the product market and the absence of stockholder control. Hence, the question of control over monopoly power can be transformed from a logical one to an empirical one. The evidence in Chapters 6 and 7 has some relevance to the evaluation of this question.

3. Summary

Treating all revisions to the theory of the firm as the universe, the space was first divided into normative and positive sectors, and it was indicated that the present analysis belongs to the latter. Within the positive sector, a further breakdown into "realism in process" and "realism in motivation" was made, and again this analysis belongs to the latter. Having established this general framework, some of the contributions to the realism-in-motivation literature were examined, and I indicated in what respects the approach taken here is responsive to them. In particular, Gordon's views on the importance of personal goals and the role of profit as a performance constraint are largely reflected in the proposed model. Similarly, Papandreou's views on rationality, the need for a general preference function, and his concern over the problem of social choice are given specific content. Bowen's suggestion that the motivational foundations of the theory of the firm be re-examined is the object of attention in the next chapter, and his stress on the study of particular behavior within the business firm is reflected in the empirical analyses of Chapters 6 and 7.

Although Simon's emphasis on substituting adaptive for maximizing assumptions has gone unheeded, his related suggestion that personal goals be made an integral part of the theory of the firm has been accepted. Kaysen is similarly concerned with the influence of discretion on a wider range of social and economic relationships than are investigated here. Nevertheless, his use of an acceptable level profit goal, his interchangeable use of the terms management and firm, and his concern over the effects of discretion on efficiency, stability, and equity are all considered in the chapters that follow.

Although the particular model that Becker uses in his study of discrimination did not suggest any obvious ways for handling the aspects of behavior under investigation here, his use of maximizing assumptions and his insistence that conventional economic analysis can be made to have relevance for studying the effects of nonpecuniary motivation are reflected in the procedures that I employ. The Alchian–Kessel verbal description of behavior in regulated industries is similar to the discussion of emoluments in Chapter 3. However, their restriction of the argument to the public utility sector rests on a competition in the capital market argument that is not entirely convincing on a priori grounds alone.

Indeed, it appears that intended a priori grounds for establishing the superiority of the profit maximization hypothesis generally depend on additional assumptions of an empirical nature. Thus, profit is not obviously identical with utility, economic natural selection does not necessarily apply in the monopoly sector, and the competition in the capital market argument seems to depend on a mechanism for transferring monopoly that may fail to reach the source of control over that power.

In the absence of acceptable a priori arguments for establishing profit maximization as the appropriate behavioral assumption, recourse to a different line of investigation is required. The superiority of the profit maximization assumption, as compared with alternative constructions, must rest on factual rather than logical grounds. Thus the questions become: What alternative behavioral assumptions are proposed? What are their implications? And what does the evidence support?

CHAPTER 3

Organizational Behavior

As Thompson has observed, "the behavior of people in organizations is purposive in two senses. First, behavior must be minimally oriented to a common organizational purpose, or it would not be meaningful to speak of an organization. Secondly, behavior within organizations is oriented to personal goals" [126, p. 81]. The theory of the firm has traditionally recognized only the first of these—or, to the extent that the importance of personal goals has been acknowledged, these have seldom been made to have an explicit influence on the analysis. Indeed, even the minimally oriented organizational purpose of earning positive profits has generally been displaced by the assumption that firms are operated so as to maximize profits.

The objective of this chapter is to combine personal goals with a less severe statement of organizational purpose to obtain a somewhat more general basis for examining firm behavior. The motivational assumptions are stated in Section 1. The notion of "expense preference" is introduced in Section 2 in order to provide economic content to these motivational considerations.

1. Managerial Motivation

As Haire has pointed out, psychologists have largely neglected the motivation of managers [59, p. 190]. Rather than tie their analysis of motivation to particular roles, psychologists have preferred a more broadly based approach. Certainly for purposes of obtaining an overview of human behavior this is sensible. However, this is a disadvantage for the present analysis since, out of the host of factors that influence the behavior of the individual in all of his capacities, only a subset is likely to be of major importance for understanding his behavior as a manager. Hence, comprehensive lists of motives that make no effort at partitioning according to function are somewhat less than satisfactory.

That a partitioning of motives according to role is appropriate derives from the propositions that (1) not every social situation which the individual encounters is equally efficient in satisfying each particular need[1] and (2) satisfaction of a need in one capacity (for example, as a manager) has spillover value to other capacities (for example, as a head of a household). Rational behavior, therefore, requires that the individual discriminate in his attempts to achieve need satisfaction. In one environment he will seek satisfaction for one group of needs, in another environment he will seek satisfaction for a second group of needs, and so forth. This selective pursuit of goals means that we can properly limit the analysis of behavior in any one environmental sector to that subset of goals that is immediately relevant in that sector.[2]

The criteria for selection of goals to be included in the subset are two: What satisfactions is the environment particularly well-suited to satisfy? What needs does the environment create? Armed with these criteria one can proceed to identify those individual objectives that will receive attention in each particular situation.

Considering the limited psychological commitment made by the classical theory of the firm, significant improvement in the behavioral content of the theory may be possible by making only simple changes in the character of the assumptions. Looking at the immediate, rather than the ultimate determinants of managerial behavior, may be sufficient for this purpose. A substantial consensus exists among organization theorists and economists who have carefully studied the operations of the business firm on what constitutes the "immediate determinants of

---

[1] This basis for limiting the class of needs that require attention was suggested to me by Professor J. G. March.

[2] Although a degree of overlapping is to be expected, as long as the intersection of the subsets is smaller than their union selective goal pursuit of the sort suggested can be expected to occur.

behavior." The following matrix displays the major elements that enter this consensus.[3]

	Salary	Security	Status	Power	Prestige	Social Service	Professional Excellence
Barnard[1]	x	x	x	x	x	x	x
Cole[2]		x		x	x	x	
Gordon[3]	x	x	x	x	x	x	x
Simon[4]	x		x	x	x		
Thompson[5]	x	x	x	x	x		

[1] See [9, pp. x, xi, 139, 142–49, 159, 221] and [10].
[2] See [32, p. 16].
[3] See [54, pp. xii, 272, 283, 305–16].
[4] See [113, pp. 114–18].
[5] See [126, pp. 22, 68–69, 93].

---

[3] In addition to the factors listed, Barnard and Simon include expansion as an objective of the firm. However, as the subsequent analysis shows, expansion is less an objective in itself than it is a means to the attainment of salary, security, power, status, and prestige. Moreover, it is not a general expansion of the entire scale of the enterprise that is desired, but a selective expansion of the expenditures that most contribute to managerial satisfactions. If indeed the argument that expansion is not an end but instead is a principal means to the attainment of other objectives is correct, and if the resulting expansion occurs in a selective rather than general way, it seems misleading to treat expansion as an additional objective.

Barnard also places great emphasis on the "moral responsibility" of executive position and argues that this "process of inculcating [organizational] points of view . . . will result in subordinating individual interest . . . to the good of the cooperative whole" [9, p. 279]. Although this is surely correct, it does not mean that the motives listed above are of no consequence. Rather, these individual objectives are moderated by organizational influences. The analysis in Chapter 8 examines some of the organizational factors that are responsible for these socialization effects.

Obviously the objectives are not independent, and to some extent their number can be reduced.[4] For example, status, power, and prestige can be approximately represented by the notion of *dominance*.[5] Since, however, the triplet (status, power, prestige) is more descriptive than the composite term (dominance), and as there may be differences in the behavior that each of the elements produces, I shall continue to use the three terms—either separately or in combination—as well as the composite term. Moreover, salary is not a "motive" in the same sense as the other factors listed. Instead, salary might be interpreted more as a means to the attainment of security, status, power, and prestige than as an independent source of activity.[6] However, material reward is an activity that the business firm is exceptionally well-suited to provide and to subsume salary in these other motives tends to conceal this important relationship. Therefore, rather than represent it by these other motives and risk the loss of this connection, salary is retained as a separate objective.

Relative to opportunities available in other environmental situations, the opportunity to attend to social service objections in the business firm is probably not great. Moreover, the effect it has on business behavior has never been well-defined. Is it responsible for business contributions to educational and eleemosynary institutions, or can these be explained, as Alchian and Kessel do [2, p. 167], as attempts to acquire status, prestige, and goodwill for the management and the firm? Probably a combination of these factors is working. Nonetheless, as long as "social service" considerations fail to give rise to activity that significantly differs in kind from these other motives, the analysis will be simplified by eliminating it.

---

[4] The terms are used in a conventional sense. The following definitions, which have generally been taken from *Webster's New Collegiate Dictionary* (2nd ed.), convey the meaning intended to be associated with each.

salary: pecuniary compensation paid regularly;

security: feeling of assurance of safety; freedom from anxiety;

status: a position of affairs;

power: the possession of controlling influence over others;

prestige: ascendancy derived from general esteem;

social service: performance of office for the benefit of society;

professional excellence: superior operating performance or technical improvement of the profession.

[5] Indeed, Stagner and Karwoski discuss dominance explicitly in these terms [118, pp. 118–20].

[6] Surely it can be assumed that the basic physiological needs of the managers are adequately fulfilled, so that salary is irrelevant to these needs.

We thus emerge with the following list of motives:

1. Salary.
2. Security.
3. Dominance:
    (a) status,
    (b) power,
    (c) prestige.
4. Professional excellence.

Motives 1 and 4, salary and professional excellence, clearly fall under the grouping referred to above as satisfactions the business firm is well-suited to satisfy. Indeed, there may be little opportunity for the pursuit of either of these outside of the organization. Motive 2, security, reflects attention to needs that the environment creates. To the extent that instability and uncertainty characterize the environment, security needs will receive more attention. Motive 3, dominance, is included because activity in the organization provides opportunities to satisfy status, power, and prestige and because the organization creates needs for these attainments. Hence, it satisfies both parts of our criterion for inclusion.

In terms of Maslow's hierarchy of needs—physiological, safety, love, esteem, and self-actualization [85]—salary bears no exact relation, but security roughly overlaps the safety and love needs, dominance is an esteem need, and professional excellence is a variety of self-actualization. Maslow argues that higher order needs become activated only when the lower order needs are satisfied. According to this view, environmental conditions will have a profound influence on the needs to which managers attend. In general, managers operating firms in the monopolistic sector should have relatively more opportunity to become sated with respect to security and dominance needs and, hence, give more attention to professional objectives than would managers in the competitive sector. Indeed, social service objectives may even become operative in regulated industries, such as public utilities and communications, where the pressures of competition are legally restrained and the incentives to engage in nonprofit activities may be substantial (see Chapter 4).

2. Expense Preference and Organizational Policy Formation

A listing of goals is only a first step toward a reformulation of the motivational assumptions in the theory of the firm. Indeed, that other studies of managerial behavior have frequently stopped short of providing economic content to their observations is probably due to the failure to take the critical second step: namely, to identify the *means* by which objectives can be satisfied. The notion of *expense preference* is developed in Section 2.1 for the purpose of making the connection between motives and economic activity. This is then followed by a discussion of organizational policy formation in Section 2.2.

2.1. Expense Preference. Pigou defines the scope of economics as "that part of social welfare that can be brought directly or indirectly into relation with the measuring-rod of money" [93, p. 11]. Indeed, considering the analytical difficulties of imposing a metric on security, status, power, or prestige, the advantage of interpreting behavior in monetary terms should be obvious. The desirability of transforming these nonpecuniary objectives into pecuniary terms therefore suggests itself. The notion of "expense preference" is used to perform this transformation. Such an indirect approach seems to correspond to Marshall's observation that although "desires cannot be measured directly," they can be measured "by the outward phenomena to which they give rise" [83, p. 92].

By expense preference I mean that managers do not have a neutral attitude toward all classes of expenses. Instead, some types of expenses have positive values attached to them: they are incurred not merely for their contributions to productivity (if any) but, in addition, for the manner in which they enhance the individual and collective objectives of managers. Conventional economic theory treats all expenses symmetrically: individuals are indifferent toward costs of all types. Expense preference replaces this attitude of indifference by positive tastes for certain classes of expenses. Asymmetry thus develops in the attitude toward costs.

Although the resulting model is expressed entirely in monetary units, it should not be interpreted as one in which pecuniary goals are the only objectives of the firm. Rather, the nonpecuniary goals indicated above are manifested through the mechanism of expense preference, and in this way are assumed to influence the operation of the firm in systematic and predictable ways.

It should be emphasized, however, that the connections described below for relating motives to behavior *are assumed*. They appear to be plausible and the argument attempts to demonstrate this plausibility. Whether the connections claimed are accurate can only be established by investigation. Although the evidence that is examined in Chapters 6 and 7 has an indirect bearing on this question, it bears directly only

on the expenses for which a positive preference is claimed. It is possible
that the positive association that appears to exist between these expense
levels and discretion is due to reasons other than those described. It is
also possible that there are other expenses for which a preference exists
that have not been identified. Finally, it is possible that the motives
considered above are incomplete. These are separate issues on which
the evidence does not yield definitive answers. In general, they are
beyond the range of the present investigation; they lie mainly in the
field of psychology.

2.1.1. Staff. It is assumed that the management has a positive expense
preference for staff. Roughly this corresponds to general administrative
and selling expense.

As Marshall observed, the selective expansion of operations may
easily be perceived by the management as having benefits that can be
distributed quite generally throughout the management hierarchy [84,
pp. 321–22]. Indeed, since promotional opportunities within a fixed-size
firm are limited (while to increase jurisdiction has the same general
effect as promotion but simultaneously produces the opportunity for
advance to all [113, pp. 117–18] [126, pp. 101–2]), the incentive to
expand staff may be difficult to resist. Being a means to promotion,
expansion of staff serves to advance both salary and dominance objectives simultaneously. In addition, staff can contribute to the satisfaction
of security and professional achievement objectives as well [9, p. 159].

Organization theorists have observed that "the modern organization
is a prolific generator of anxiety and insecurity" [126, p. 24]. This insecurity is partly due to uncertainty with respect to the survival of the
organization as a whole and more importantly (and more immediately
relevant to its individual members), of the parts with which the individuals identify. Attempts to reduce this condition can be expected.
Indeed, the direction these efforts will take can be anticipated. If the
surest guarantee of the survival of the individual parts appears to be
size, efforts to expand the separate staff functions can be predicted.

The "professional" inducement to expand staff arises from the typical
view that a progressive staff is one that is continuously providing more
and better services. An aggressive staff will therefore be looking for
ways to expand. Although in choosing directions for expansion the relative contribution to productivity will be considered the absolute effect
on profit may be neglected. As long as the organization is able to satisfy
its acceptable level performance requirements, the tendency to value

staff apart from reasons associated with its productivity produces a pre-
disposition to extend programs beyond the point where marginal costs
equal marginal benefits.

2.1.2. Emoluments. The term emoluments is used in a somewhat special
sense. It refers to that *portion* of management salaries and perquisites
that is discretionary. That is, emoluments represent rewards which, if
removed, would not cause the managers to seek other employment.
They are economic rents and have associated with them zero produc-
tivities. They are not a return to entrepreneurial capacity but instead
result from the strategic advantage that the management possesses in
the distribution of returns to monopoly power. Being a source of material
satisfaction and an indirect source of status and prestige, they are
desirable as a means for satisfying goals in each of these respects.

Tax considerations aside, the management would normally prefer to
take these emoluments as salary rather than as perquisites of office since
taken as salary, there are no restrictions on the way in which they are
spent whereas, if withdrawn as corporate personal consumption (such
as expense accounts, executive services, office suites, and so forth), there
are specific limitations on the ways these can be enjoyed. However, there
are two considerations that make perquisites attractive: first, for tax
purposes it may be advantageous to withdraw some part of discretionary
funds as perquisites rather than salary; second, perquisites are much
less visible rewards to the management than salary and hence are less
likely to provoke stockholder or labor dissatisfaction.[7] Hence a division
of emoluments between salary and perquisites is to be expected.

Although it is difficult to specify what fraction of salary and perquisites are discretionary in the sense defined, it is possible, as is shown in
Chapters 6 and 7, to test for the relation of these rewards to competition
in the product market and managerial tastes. Thus, they can be identified
ex post even if not *ex ante*.

2.1.3. Discretionary Profit. As was indicated at the beginning of this
chapter, positive profits constitute the "minimally oriented organizational purpose." Thus, zero profits place a lower bound on what is con-

---

[7] Historically, whenever stockholder discontent has been rampant, management
compensation has been a favorite target [54, p. 164]. Likewise in wage negotiations,
unions often make a point of executive salary levels. Perquisites, being much less
visible, are less readily attacked.

sistent with survival, whereas maximum profits place an upper bound on what is attainable. Under some circumstances the range between these two may be narrow. Typically this will be the case when competitors are numerous and entry is easy. Under other circumstances, a broader range may exist.

As was indicated in Chapter 2, the stockholders may frequently lack sufficient information, organized power, and determination to compel the management to maximize profits. However, they are not totally ignorant, completely fractionated, or entirely passive. Thus they will ordinarily be in a position to mobilize their forces should profits fall below some minimum acceptable level (and in this they may be joined by the firm's creditors). The precise determination of this level involves the interaction of the relative performance of rivals, the historical performance of the firm, and special current conditions that affect the firm's performance. If it can be assumed that the stockholders will actively attempt to intervene in the affairs of the firm whenever the acceptable level is violated, then, by observing the magnitude of the changes in profitability required to stimulate general dissatisfaction, a crude estimate of the severity of the minimum profit constraint can be obtained. Since these changes generally appear to be large, it can be inferred that the acceptable level usually represents only modest attainment.

I define as "discretionary profit" that amount by which earnings exceed this minimum performance constraint. That the managers should desire to earn profits that exceed the acceptable level derives from the relationship that profit bears to discretion, self-fulfillment, and organizational achievement. Since expansion of staff and emoluments can scarcely proceed independently of the expansion of physical facilities, and since financing of this expansion (whether from internal or external sources) will be tied to profitability of the firm, profits in excess of the minimum acceptable level may well be desired by the management. Moreover, managers derive satisfaction from self-fulfillment and organizational achievement and profit is one measure of this success. Taken together, these considerations favor the inclusion of a profit component in the firm's preference function.

2.2. Organizational Policy Formation. Modern organization theory has tended to treat the firm as a coalition (managers, workers, stockholders, suppliers, customers), the members of which have conflicting demands which must be reconciled if the firm is to remain a going concern [81, Chap. 4] [108]. In the sense that each group in the coalition is essential to the firm's continuing existence, the coalition can be considered as one in which the members are "equals." This view, however, is more useful when observing the firm in a period of crisis than one in which survival is not a pressing problem.

Where survival is not a current concern, restoring a hierarchy among the members based on the attention they give to the firm's operations may lead to more productive insights. From this viewpoint, management emerges as the chief member of the coalition: its role as the coordinating and initiating agent as well as its preferred access to information permit it quite naturally to assume this position of primacy. Thus, although in certain circumstances it is necessary to give special attention to shifts in demands made by members of the coalition other than managers, under "normal" conditions it may be entirely appropriate to take the demands of the other members (for wages, profits, product, etc.) as *given* and leave it to the discretion of the management to operate the firm in some best sense.

I formulate the models in the following chapter precisely in this fashion. That is, it is assumed that the firm is operated so as to maximize a utility function that has as principal components, staff, emoluments, and discretionary profit, subject to the constraint that reported profit be greater than or equal to the minimum acceptable level of profit demanded.

3. Conclusion

As Bronfenbrenner has noted in commenting on the Alchian-Kessel treatment of nonpecuniary goals, "these propositions are ... more or less obvious. Simply raising them among one's friends with or without professional training in economics will suffice to show how obvious they are" [27, p. 180]. The self-evident nature of these notions makes it somewhat difficult to express them in a nontrivial way and tends to produce the reaction "so what?"

It is my objective in the remainder of this treatise to respond to this challenge by (1) demonstrating that nonpecuniary motives can be introduced into a formal model using the notion of expense preference stated above; (2) developing the equilibrium and comparative statics properties of the resulting model and comparing these to alternative constructions; and (3) examining the evidence that bears on the validity of the models. This completed, the "so what" query can be evaluated from more solid ground.

CHAPTER 4

A Morphology of Models of the Business Firm: I, Managerial Discretion Models

The preceding chapters have reviewed the kinds of suggestions for modifying the theory of the firm that have been made in the past 15 years, examined possible limitations of the profit maximization assumption, and suggested an alternative motivational foundation that would appear to be generally consistent with managerial behavior (broadly conceived). The objective now is to develop a model that is responsive to some of the criticisms of the classical theory of the firm by providing analytical content to the motivational assumptions given in Chapter 3. This involves the construction of utility functions for the firm that make the notion of "expense preference" explicit. Invoking the assumption of maximizing behavior, equilibrium and comparative statics properties of the models are obtained.

Since the results are best put in perspective by comparing them with those obtained from alternative models—in particular, those of the traditional theory of the firm—parallel operations are performed on two versions of the profit maximizing model. These appear in the following chapter. The first is the usual or single-period profit maximizing model. Next, a discounted or multi-period profit maximization model is constructed. The latter is important both because it avoids the *ad hoc* treatment frequently accorded to long-run profit maximization and because it makes more severe the problem of discriminating between the utility maximizing and profit maximizing hypotheses. That is, certain of the implications of the utility maximization analysis are also obtained from the multi-period profit maximizing model that do not occur under the usual short-run formulation.

To complete the morphology of models of the business firm, Baumol's sales maximization hypothesis is also examined. A parallel treatment of the equilibrium and comparative statics properties is performed. Again some overlap exists between the implications of this model and those of the managerial discretion models and the profit maximization hypothesis.

1. Managerial Discretion Models of the Business Firm

1.1. General Properties of the Models. Managerial discretion models of the business firm are intended to apply to firms where competitive conditions are not typically severe and where the management may therefore enjoy significant discretion in developing its strategy. The underlying motivational assumptions for these models have been developed in Chapter 3. They require that the firm's preference function be extended to include certain expense components in addition to the usual profit term.

The most fundamental type of expense preference, at least with respect to its effect on comparative statics properties and possibly with respect to its effect on expenditures as well, is the positive preference that managers display toward staff. The implications of introducing staff into the objective function of the firm are examined in the first of the discretion models.

A second variety of expense preference is the desire of managers to spend some portion of actual profit earned on emoluments—on discretionary additions to salary and on corporate personal consumption. The implications of introducing an emoluments term into the firm's preference function are developed in the second of the discretion models.

Emoluments and staff components are both included in the utility function of the firm in the third model. Although profit is included as one of the objectives sought by the management of the firm in each of the three models examined, it is not merely profit per se but also the discretion that it provides that makes profit desirable to the management. To make this clear, the descriptive expression "discretionary profit" is used rather than the more precise expression "the algebraic difference between reported (after tax) profit and minimum profit demanded" to identify this profit term.

The following terms enter into the analysis:

$$R = \text{revenue} = PX; \; \partial^2 R/\partial X \partial S \geq 0$$
$$P = \text{price} = P(X, S; E); \; \partial P/\partial X < 0; \; \partial P/\partial S \geq 0;$$
$$\partial P/\partial E > 0$$
$$X = \text{output}$$
$$S = \text{staff (in money terms), or (approximately) general}$$
administrative and selling expense
$$E = \text{the condition of the environment (a demand shift}$$
parameter)
$$C = \text{production cost} = C(X)$$
$$M = \text{managerial emoluments}$$
$$\pi = \text{actual profit} = R - C - S$$
$$\pi_R = \text{reported profit} = \pi - M$$
$$\pi_0 = \text{minimum (after tax) profit demanded}$$
$$T = \text{taxes, where } t = \text{tax rate and } \bar{T} = \text{lump-sum tax}$$
$$\pi_R - \pi_0 - T = \text{discretionary profit}$$
$$U = \text{the utility function}$$

1.2. The Staff Model. With staff and discretionary profit entering into the utility function, the firm's objective is taken to be

$$\text{maximize:} \quad U = U(S, \pi - \pi_0 - T)$$

$$\text{subject to:} \quad \pi \geq \pi_0 + T$$

The constraint can be rewritten as $\pi - \pi_0 - T \geq 0$. Assuming diminishing marginal utility and disallowing corner solutions, it follows that the firm will always choose values of its decision variables that will yield positive utility with respect to each component of its utility function. The second component is $\pi - \pi_0 - T$. If it is always to be positive, then the constraint will always be satisfied as an inequality. Thus the constraint is redundant and the problem can be treated as one of straightforward maximization.[1] Substituting the functional relationships for profits into the expression yields:

$$\text{maximize:} \quad U = U[S, (1 - t)(R - C - S - \bar{T}) - \pi_0]$$

---

[1] Although this is a convenience, it is by no means a necessity. Thus, an inequality constrained maximization problem can be handled by making use of the Kuhn-Tucker theorem [76].

The following first-order results are obtained by setting the partial derivatives of U with respect to X and S equal to zero.[2]

(1)
$$\frac{\partial R}{\partial X} = \frac{\partial C}{\partial X}$$

(2)
$$\frac{\partial R}{\partial S} = \frac{-U_1 + (1 - t)U_2}{(1 - t)U_2}$$

From Equation 1 we observe that the firm makes its production decision in the conventional fashion by equating marginal gross revenue to the marginal costs of production. However, Equation 2 reveals that the firm will employ staff in the region where the marginal value product of staff is less than its marginal cost. That is, the firm will operate where $\partial R/\partial S < 1$, whereas the usual short-period profit maximization model would employ staff only to the point where the equality between marginal costs and benefits obtains. Equation 2 can be rewritten as

$$\frac{\partial R}{\partial S} = 1 - \frac{1}{1 - t}\frac{U_1}{U_2}$$

where U_1/U_2 is the marginal rate of substitution between profit and staff. *Ceteris paribus*, an increase in the ratio reflects a shift in tastes in favor of staff. In a profit maximizing organization this ratio is zero.

These relationships are displayed graphically in Figure 1. With staff plotted along the ordinate and output along the abscissa, isoprofit contours are imbedded in the XS plane. These contours are elliptical with major axes running from southwest to northeast.[3] Connecting points of tangency between the isoprofit contours and a series of horizontal lines at successively greater levels of staff traces out the locus $R_x = C_x$—i.e., the locus of optimal output given the level of staff expense. Similarly the points of tangency between the isoprofit contours and a series of

---

[2] In these expressions, U_1 is the first partial of the utility function with respect to S and U_2 is the first partial with respect to $(1 - t)(R - C - S - \bar{T}) - \pi_0$.

[3] That this is the correct relationship follows from the assumption that $\partial^2 R/\partial X \partial S > 0$. Under this assumption, the effect of increasing staff is to shift the marginal revenue curve of the standard price-quantity demand curve to the right so that necessarily, whatever the shape of the marginal cost of production curve, the optimum output increases as staff increases. To preserve this property in the construction of an isoprofit map on the output-staff plane requires that the isoprofit curves have major axes running from southwest to northeast. See n. 5, p. 44 for further discussion of the sign of $\partial^2 R/\partial X \partial S$.

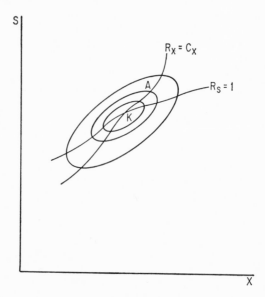

Figure 1

vertical lines drawn at successively greater levels of output yields the
locus $R_s = 1$. Their intersection, K, corresponds to the short-run profit
maximization position.

Since the equilibrium relations are $R_x = C_x$ and $R_s < 1$, the utility
maximizing firm will take up a position somewhere along the locus
$R_x = C_x$ but above the locus $R_s = 1$. Point A in Figure 1 represents
such a position. Thus, the utility maximizing firm will choose a larger
value of staff, and this will in turn give rise to a larger value of output
than would be chosen by the firm that maximizes short-run profit.

The locus $R_x = C_x$ specifies the pairs of (X, S) combinations along
which the firm that has its utility function augmented to include a
staff component will locate. For every value of staff there exists an
optimal value of output, say $\hat{X}$, where $\hat{X} = f(S)$. Given the condition
of the environment, profit depends on the choice of X and S, that is,
$\pi = g(X, S; E)$. If, however, X is chosen optimally, then

$$\pi = g(\hat{X}, S; E) = g[f(S), S; E] = g'(S; E)$$

Thus, profit can be plotted as a function of staff. This is done in Figure
2 with profit along the ordinate and staff along the abscissa. By introducing indifference curves between profit and staff, the equilibrium
results can be interpreted somewhat differently. Again, the point K

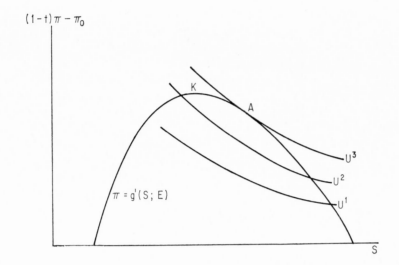

$(1-t)\pi - \pi_0$

K

A

U^3

U^2

U^1

$\pi = g'(S\,;\,E)$

S

Figure 2

represents the profit maximizing position and A, the point where the tangency between the indifference curves and the profits curve obtains, is the position at which the utility maximizing firm will locate.

Several generalizations suggest themselves immediately. First, for the firm to select the point K requires that the slope of the indifference curves in the region around K be zero; that is, the marginal rate of substitution between profits and staff must be zero. Since

$$\text{MRS} = -\frac{d\pi}{dS} = \frac{\partial U/\partial S}{\partial U/\partial \pi},$$ this implies that the marginal utility of staff

in the vicinity of K must be zero. Either staff must be "objectively" valued only for its contribution to profit or the benefits associated with expanding staff must be exhausted before K is reached. If the argument regarding the positive preference for staff is accepted, the first of these can be dismissed and the second represents a limiting condition. Considering the variety of ways in which staff contributes to managerial satisfactions, the zero marginal utility condition seems unlikely to be realized.

A second observation is that if the profit curve is very sharply peaked, the resulting tangency will be one where the value of staff (and output) selected will not be far removed from the profit maximization position. As the profit curve becomes flatter, however, and as the indifference curves become more steeply sloped (i.e., as staff becomes relatively more highly valued), the tangency shifts progressively to the right.

Having established the equilibrium conditions, the comparative statics properties of the model remain to be developed. That is, we want to displace the equilibrium. In particular, we want to find how the system adjusts to a change in the condition of the environment (the demand shift parameter E), a change in the profit tax rate (t), and a lump-sum tax $(\bar{T})$.

It will facilitate the argument to compact the notation and designate each decision variable by Z_i and each parameter by α_j. Then the function $U(X, S; E, t, \bar{T})$ can be represented as $U(Z_1, Z_2; \alpha_1, \alpha_2, \alpha_3)$. The general form[4] for determining the response of the pth decision variable to a change in the kth parameter is:

$$
\left(\frac{\partial Z_p}{\partial \alpha_k}\right)^0 = \frac{-\sum_{i=1}^{2}\dfrac{\partial^2 U}{\partial Z_i \partial \alpha_k}D_{ip}}{|D|}, \qquad \begin{array}{l} p = 1, 2 \\ k = 1, \ldots, 3 \end{array}
$$

where D_{ip} is the cofactor of the ith row and the pth column of D and $|D|$ is the determinant of the second partials $\partial^2 U/\partial Z_i \partial Z_j$. The sign matrix D is

$$
D = \left\| \begin{array}{cc} - & + \\ + & - \end{array} \right\|
$$

Second-order conditions for a maximum require that D be positive.[5]

---

[4] See Samuelson [99, pp. 12–14].

[5] If D is an $n \times n$ matrix, second-order stability conditions for a maximum require that the principal minors alternate in sign beginning with a negative. It might be noted that I assign $\partial^2 U/\partial X \partial S$ a positive sign in the D matrix. This follows from my assumption that $\partial^2 R/\partial X \partial S$ is positive. From a strictly theoretical standpoint it is not essential that this be positive in order to preserve stability. All that is necessary is that the 2×2 matrix be negative definite. From a practical standpoint, however, it is difficult to imagine how $\partial^2 R/\partial X \partial S$ could be anything other than positive (or, as a limiting condition, when the effects of staff on price are exhausted, zero). That is, as output increases, staff unchanged, we would generally expect that the change in gross revenue that would obtain from increasing staff incrementally would be larger than the corresponding change that would occur at lower values of output. This same assumption is made in the profit maximization models examined in the following chapter. If the demand function is multiplicative, $\partial^2 U/\partial X \partial S$ will be positive unambiguously.

The signs of the values $\partial^2 U/\partial Z_i \partial \alpha_k$ for $Z_i = X,\ S$ and $\alpha_k = E,\ t,\ \bar{T}$ are as follows:[6]

$$
\left\| \frac{\partial^2 U}{\partial Z_i \partial \alpha_k} \right\| = \begin{array}{c c c c} & E & t & \bar{T} \\ X & + & 0 & 0 \\ S & + & +? & - \end{array}
$$

The comparative statics responses, shown in Table 1, are obtained directly and without difficulty from the sign relationships alone. The

TABLE 1. COMPARATIVE STATICS RESPONSES FOR THE STAFF MODEL

		Parameter		
		E	t	$\bar{T}$
Variable	X^0	+	+?	−
	S^0	+	+?	−

direction of adjustment of any particular decision variable to a displacement from equilibrium by an increase in a parameter is found by referring to the row and column entry corresponding to this pair.

That the response to an increase in the profits tax rate is not unambiguous is due to a combination of substitution and income effects. As shown in Appendix 4-A, the net substitution effect of staff to an increase in the profits tax rate is always positive, whereas the "income" effect is always negative. The gross substitution effect is the combination of these two separate effects so that its sign depends on their relative magnitudes. As shown in Appendix 4-A, the gross substitution effect will usually be positive although, when the firm encounters adversity and has difficulty in satisfying its minimum profit constraint, the response

---

[6] Although the sign of $\partial^2 U/\partial X \partial E$ is certain to be positive as indicated, I need to appeal to a "reasonableness" argument to assign a positive sign to $\partial^2 U/\partial S \partial E$. The argument, very simply, is that as the environment moves from a buyers' market to a sellers' market (i.e., as E increases), an incremental increase in staff activity yields a larger increase in gross revenue than the same increment would have produced under less favorable environmental conditions. The results are unaffected if $\partial^2 U/\partial S \partial E$ is zero but ambiguities develop if $\partial^2 U/\partial S \partial E$ is permitted to become negative. In this case, the model has to be specialized and particular demand and cost expressions introduced. These same qualifications with respect to the sign of $\partial^2 U/\partial S \partial E$ hold for the profit maximization models examined in the following chapter.

may be negative. The direction of response of output to a change in the profits tax rate is identical to that of staff. Indeed, it is a derived rather than a direct effect: in the absence of the staff component in the utility function, output would be unchanged.

These income and substitution effects can also be interpreted graphically by an extension of the apparatus used in Figure 2. In the construction of that figure it was shown that $\pi = g'(S)$. It is likewise true, therefore, that $(1 - t)\pi - \pi_0$ can be expressed as a function of staff, where $(1 - t)\pi - \pi_0$ is discretionary profit (Figure 3).

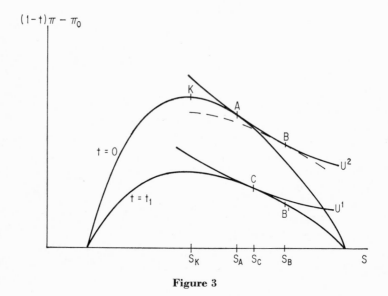

Figure 3

The profit as a function of staff curves are drawn for a tax rate of $t = 0$ and $t = t_1$, where $t_1 > 0$. At tax rate $t = 0$, the optimum position for the firm occurs at A, where tangency between the profits curve $t = 0$ and the indifference curve U^2 occurs. When the tax rate is increased to t_1, tangency of the resulting profit curve and the indifference curves occurs at C. As drawn, the optimal choice of staff increases ($S_C > S_A$).

The adjustment can be broken up into an income and a substitution effect by introducing a *compensated* tax change. Thus the dashed curve through A is a vertical displacement of the curve $t = t_1$. If the firm were awarded a lump-sum bounty simultaneously with the increase in the profits tax just large enough for it to continue to realize the utility represented by U^2, its profit curve would be the dashed curve shown. Since the slope of the curve t_1 is everywhere less than the corresponding slope of the curve $t = 0$, tangency between the dashed curve and the indifference curves will occur to the right of A. The point designated B represents such a position, and the shift from A to B is the *net substitution effect*. Since profit and staff are substitutes, the net substitution effect is unambiguously positive; that is, when the "price" of taking satisfaction in the form of profit increases, the compensated tax adjustment always leads to a substitution of staff for profit and $S_B > S_A$.

If the indifference curves were vertical displacements of one another, the curve U^1 would be tangent to the profits curve $t = t_1$ at B'. The vertical displacement condition, however, is not quite realistic. It represents a condition where, given the level of staff, the marginal rate of substitution across successive indifference curves is constant. Instead, the marginal rate of substitution will normally fall as profit declines. That is, at lower levels of profit, the increase in staff required to offset a specified reduction in profit and still maintain the same level of utility becomes larger. Thus the indifference curve U^1 is drawn so that the marginal rate of substitution at each level of staff is everywhere smaller than it is along the indifference curve U^2. Hence tangency occurs not at B' but at C. The shift from B to C represents the *income effect*. Were the vertical displacement condition to hold between indifference curves, the income effect would be zero. In the usual circumstance where the marginal rate of substitution falls as profit declines, the income effect will be negative and $S_C < S_B$.

By postulating that the marginal rate of substitution behaves in this prescribed way instead of permitting it to vary without limitation, I impose a restriction on the utility function that may seem objectionable. I submit, however, that the restriction is perfectly reasonable. It merely guarantees that the staff component in the utility function is not an inferior good. Whereas special assumptions of this sort are unwarranted in the analysis of consumer behavior where the arguments that enter the utility function are deliberately left in an unspecified general form (and hence the possibility of inferior good must be admitted), the components of utility function under study here are fully specified and, hence, the analysis can be bounded appropriately. Indeed, where generality is attained only at the expense of relevance, a specialization of the analysis that removes uninteresting or implausible contingencies is altogether warranted.

Invoking this principle in the present case dictates the following choice: since each of the expenses for which a positive preference has been indicated is surely a normal good and since leaving the inferior good possibility open merely produces confusion, the inferior good contingency is disallowed. Indeed, Scitovsky's analysis of entrepreneurial behavior is essentially an application of this principle and rests on a stronger specialization of the utility function than the one I employ. In his analysis the marginal rate of substitution, given the level of activity, is constant across successive levels of profit (see n. 6 in Chapter 2, p. 18). In the present analysis, this constant marginal rate of substitution relationship represents a limiting condition.

The gross substitution effect is the combination of the net substitution and income effects and thus depends on the relative magnitudes of these two effects. As shown in Appendix 4-A, the gross substitution effect will normally be positive ($S_C > S_A$), although as adversity is encountered and the firm is hard pressed to satisfy its minimum profit constraint, it may become negligible and could become negative. As long as the firm is enjoying comparative prosperity, however, the gross substitution effect will generally be positive and staff will be increased in response to an increase in the profits tax rate.

The effects of a progressive tax rate can be investigated by letting $T = h(\pi)$ be the profits tax. Then discretionary profit will be $\pi - h(\pi) - \pi_0$, and, since $\pi = g'(S)$, this can be expressed as a function of staff. This is shown in Figure 4, where the responses to a constant

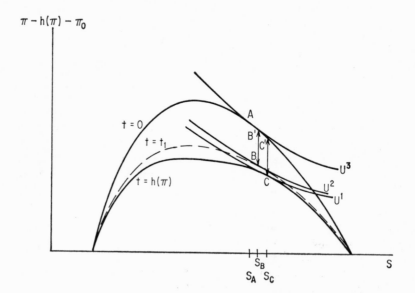

Figure 4

and progressive tax rate are examined. Three profit curves are drawn. The top curve represents a zero tax condition. The solid curve below it shows profit under a progressive profits tax. The dashed curve shows profits under a constant profits tax. The progressive tax rate produces a profit curve flatter at the top than does the constant tax rate. Thus tangency between the indifference curves and the profit curve is shifted significantly to the right (at C). Actual profit is given by C' and the distance between C and C' is the amount of tax collected.[7] To summarize, under the progressive profits tax, actual profit is reduced from π_A to $\pi_{C'}$, due to expanding staff from S_A to S_C, and a tax of CC' is collected.

The constant profits rate t_1 is chosen so that tangency between the resulting profit curve and the indifference curves occurs at a point that yields precisely the same amount of tax as was collected under the progressive tax program. Thus the length BB' is the same as CC'. Since the marginal tax rate under the constant profits tax is less than it would be under the progressive profits tax plan, there is less incentive for the firm to absorb profits and take its satisfactions through staff. Thus $S_B < S_C$, $\pi_B > \pi_C$, and $\pi_{B'} > \pi_{C'}$. These results hold over the entire range of possible progressive versus constant profits tax rates as long as tax collections under both arrangements are required to be equal.

The effects of a lump-sum tax can also be examined with this type of diagram. To increase the lump-sum tax shifts the profit curve vertically downward. If the indifference curves were vertical displacements of one another, tangency would occur at precisely the same level of staff expense. Since, however, the marginal rate of substitution decreases as profit decreases (given the level of staff), the indifference curves become somewhat flatter and tangency obtains at a lower value for staff.

As is well-known (and as is shown in Chapter 5), the short-run profit maximizing firm is entirely unresponsive to both a change in the profits tax rate as well as to the levy of a lump-sum tax. The implications of the utility maximization analysis as contrasted with those of the usual profit maximizing analysis are thus significantly different and appear to be testable.

1.2. The Emoluments Model. An emoluments term is substituted for the staff term that appeared in the preceding model. That is, management is assumed to have a positive taste for discretionary assignments

---

[7] Actual profit is given by C' only when $\pi_0 = 0$. Otherwise actual profit is given by profits at C' plus π_0. However, the value of π_0 in no way effects the general properties of the results.

of available funds for salary and perquisites, but has a neutral preference for staff. Thus the objective becomes

$$\text{maximize:} \quad U = U[M, \pi_R - \pi_0 - T]$$

$$\text{subject to:} \quad \pi_R \geq \pi_0 + T.$$

Again the constraint is redundant so that the problem can be handled as one of conventional maximization. Substituting the functional relationships for profits into the expression, the objective is to

$$\text{maximize:} \quad U = U[M, (1 - t)(R - C - S - M - \bar{T}) - \pi_0]$$

First-order conditions for an extremum are obtained by setting the partial derivatives with respect to X, S, and M equal to zero. Thus we obtain

(3)
$$\frac{\partial R}{\partial X} = \frac{\partial C}{\partial X}$$

(4)
$$\frac{\partial R}{\partial S} = 1$$

(5)
$$U_1 = (1 - t)U_2$$

From Equations 3 and 4 it follows that the firm will adopt a conventional short-run profit maximization position so that *actual* profit will be identical with maximum. That is, the firm will earn profits represented by K in Figures 1 and 2. However, Equation 5 reveals that the firm will absorb some part of actual profit as emoluments, the amount being dependent on the tax rate. Thus *reported* profit will be less than maximum by the amount withdrawn by the management as rent. Hence, the profits tax is levied against, and dividends are paid out of, earnings that are less than maximum.

The comparative statics properties of the model are found by the same procedure used for the preceding analysis. The sign matrix for the second partials of U is given by

$$D = \begin{Vmatrix} - & + & 0 \\ + & - & 0 \\ 0 & 0 & - \end{Vmatrix}$$

The signs of the values $\partial^2 U / \partial Z_i \partial \alpha_k$ for $Z_i = X, S, M$ and $\alpha_k = E, t, \bar{T}$ are

$$
\left\| \frac{\partial^2 U}{\partial Z_i \partial \alpha_k} \right\| =
\begin{array}{c c c c}
 & E & t & \bar{T} \\
X & + & 0 & 0 \\
S & + & 0 & 0 \\
M & + & +? & -
\end{array}
$$

The comparative statics responses can all be obtained from the signs of the partial derivatives of the equilibrium relations as displayed above alone. They are shown in Table 2.

TABLE 2. COMPARATIVE STATICS RESPONSES FOR THE EMOLUMENTS MODEL

		Parameter		
		E	t	$\bar{T}$
	X^0	+	0	0
Variable	S^0	+	0	0
	M^0	+	+?	−

The ambiguity of the response to an increase in the profits tax is again due to counteracting income and substitution effects (Figure 5). The initial (zero tax) equilibrium position is given by A. When a tax of t_1 is levied, the equilibrium position shifts to C. This can be separated into a net substitution and income effect by introducing a compensating variation. The dashed line is drawn parallel to the line $t = t_1$ and is tangent to the indifference curve U^2 (which passes through the initial position) at the point B. Thus the shift from A to B is the net substitution effect and, given the convexity relations shown between profit and emoluments, is always positive. The income effect is given by the shift from B to C. Since, for a given level of emoluments, the marginal rate of substitution between profit and emoluments declines as profit falls, the income effect will always be negative.

The gross substitution effect will be the combination of these two separate effects and will depend on their relative magnitudes. The argument developed in Appendix 4-A for examining the staff model carries over. Thus, the gross substitution effect can normally be expected to

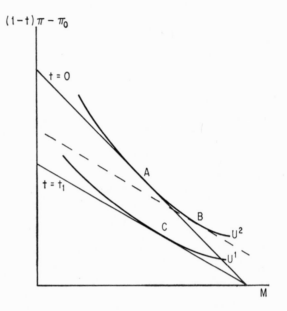

Figure 5

be positive; but as the firm approaches its minimum profit constraint, a reversal may occur.

Again it can be shown that a progressive profit tax encourages more of a substitution of emoluments for profits than would occur under a constant profits tax calculated to produce the same tax receipts. Since the argument exactly parallels that already given in the discussion of the staff model, the proof of this is omitted.

1.3. The Staff and Emoluments Model. Staff and emoluments terms are both introduced into the present model. That is, in addition to a positive preference for profit, the management of the firm also displays a positive expense preference for staff and corporate personal consumption expenditures. The objective becomes

$$\text{maximize:} \quad U = U(S, M, \pi_R - \pi_0 - T)$$

$$\text{subject to:} \quad \pi_R \geq \pi_0 + T$$

Again the constraint is redundant so that the problem can be handled as a conventional maximization one. Substituting the functional relationships for profit into the expression yields:

$$\text{maximize:} \quad U = U[S, M, (1 - t)(R - C - S - M - \bar{T}) - \pi_0]$$

First-order conditions for an extremum are obtained by setting the partial derivatives of U with respect to X, S, and M equal to zero. Thus we obtain[8]

$$(6) \qquad \frac{\partial R}{\partial X} = \frac{\partial C}{\partial X}$$

$$(7) \qquad \frac{\partial R}{\partial S} = \frac{-U_1 + (1 - t)U_3}{(1 - t)U_3}$$

$$(8) \qquad U_2 = (1 - t)U_3$$

Equation 6 reveals that the production decision is again made in a conventional profit maximizing fashion by equating marginal gross revenues to the marginal costs of production, and from Equation 7 it follows that the staff decision is again made so that the marginal value product of staff is less than its marginal cost ($R_s < 1$). Equation 8 discloses that the firm will absorb some amount of actual profit as emoluments, the amount being dependent on the tax rate.

Although the amount of profit absorbed as emoluments affects the level of discretionary profit, it has no direct influence on productivity. Thus the qualitative properties of the equilibrium of the previous models, as displayed in the figures examined earlier, likewise hold for this model.

Comparative statics properties of the model are obtained in the same way. The sign matrix of the second partials is

$$D = \begin{Vmatrix} - & + & 0 \\ + & - & -? \\ 0 & -? & - \end{Vmatrix}$$

The signs of the values $\partial^2 U/\partial Z_i \partial \alpha_k$ for $Z_i = X, S, M$ and $\alpha_k = E, t, \bar{T}$ are

$$\begin{Vmatrix} \dfrac{\partial^2 U}{\partial Z_i \partial \alpha_k} \end{Vmatrix} = \begin{matrix} & E & t & \bar{T} \\ X & + & 0 & 0 \\ S & + & +? & - \\ M & + & +? & - \end{matrix}$$

---

[8] U_1 is the first partial of the utility function with respect to S, U_2 is the first partial with respect to M, and U_3 is the first partial with respect to $(1 - t)(R - C - S - M - \bar{T}) - \pi_0$.

The sign relationships are not sufficient to derive any of the comparative statics properties for this model. This does not, however, mean that these properties are indeterminate. It only requires that the sign entries in the matrices be replaced by the functional relationships that they represent. Let d_{ij} be the element of the ith row and jth column of D. Then in d_{11} the $(-)$ term is replaced by $U_3(1 - t)(R_{xx} - C_{xx})$, in d_{12} the $(+)$ is replaced by $U_3(1 - t)R_{xs}$, and so forth. Solving the resulting system algebraically substantially eliminates the ambiguities that develop from the sign relationships alone. Thus, by replacing signs by general functional notation, wider scope for the application of qualita-

TABLE 3. COMPARATIVE STATICS RESPONSES FOR THE STAFF-EMOLUMENTS MODEL

		Parameter		
		E	t	$\bar{T}$
	X^0	+	+?	−
Variable	S^0	+	+?	−
	M^0	+	+?	−

tive economics can be claimed than Lancaster has indicated is possible [77]. This is rigorously shown in Appendix 4–B.

The comparative statics responses for this version of the managerial discretion model are shown in Table 3.

Increasing the profits tax rate again gives rise to a somewhat ambiguous response.[9] The graphical analysis of the preceding sections reveals the nature of the difficulty. As long as the firm is earning a moderate profit and the tax rate increase is not so great as to press the firm to satisfy its minimum constraint, an increase in staff, emoluments, and output can be expected. This is particularly likely if the profits tax is progressive. A reversal of these effects may occur, however, when the firm is experiencing difficulty in satisfying its minimum profit constraint.

---

[9] The responses of M to a change in each of the parameters are difficult to derive. After much manipulation, I have derived those for the profits tax and lump-sum tax unambiguously. The response to a change in the condition of the environment does not yield to this treatment. Assuming, however, that actual profit increases as demand increases (which is certainly an innocuous assumption) emoluments will also be increased as indicated.

2. General Significance of the Results

2.1. Expense Preference Reviewed. The argument in the preceding chapters has suggested that, in the absence of vigorous competition in the product market and where the separation of ownership from control is substantial, there is no compelling reason to assume that the firm is operated so as to maximize profit. On the contrary, such behavior would appear to require an unusual variety of rationality—and one not widely found in human affairs—namely, a complete detachment of individual interests from occupational decision making. A more moderate position has been suggested. Thus I proposed that where discretion in the decision-making unit exists, this will ordinarily be exercised in a fashion that reflects the individual interests of the decision makers. After reviewing the kinds of individual objectives that managers might rationally pursue it was indicated that, since most of the decision making in the firm ultimately involves spending, "expense preference" would be a useful and meaningful way in which to study the behavior of the business firm.

Two categories of expense preference were identified and related to the motives of the managers. The first of these is the positive preference for staff. The second is the positive preference for emoluments—discretionary allocations of profit for salary and perquisites. The final preference category that was identified is a profit class which, for descriptive purposes, was called discretionary profit. It has been the purpose of the preceding section of this chapter to examine the implications of such an approach by developing the equilibrium and comparative statics properties of three models which include two or more of these preference components.

2.2. Casual Empiricism as Preliminary Evidence on the Behavior of the Business Firm. Since the third model, the staff and emoluments model, incorporates all of the comparative statics responses of the preceding two, attention will be limited to it. With respect to the demand shift parameter E, this managerial model indicates that staff expenditures and output will move directly with the condition of the environment. In the limit, as the condition of the environment becomes progressively worse and the firm is pressed to satisfy its minimum profit constraint, the firm's use of staff converges to its profit maximizing value but everywhere else the firm operates where actual profit is less than maximum due to the positive preference the firm displays toward staff.

Thus spending for staff (or, approximately, general administrative and selling expense) should be highly responsive to business conditions. In general this appears to be true. Evidence that supports this is cited in Chapter 6.

In addition to the staff and output expenditures, the managerial discretion model also predicts that spending on emoluments will be responsive to the condition of the environment. Spending for these purposes will increase as conditions improve, whereas a deterioration of the environment will lead to a reversal of these profit absorption activities. Thus salaries as well as expenditures for travel, expense accounts, office improvements, and so forth, should be very much a function of business conditions. Again, this appears to conform to the facts.[10]

An increase in the profits tax rate t assigns a higher penalty to reporting profits so that an inducement exists to shift out of profit into other varieties of satisfactions. Subject to the earlier qualifications, this is exactly what the discretion model predicts. Thus, spending on both staff and emoluments increases in response to an increase in the profits tax rate. Output also increases due to the connection between optimal staff and optimal output, where an increase in the former leads to an increase in the latter.[11] Our experience with excess profits taxes appears to support this type of spending behavior.

When a lump-sum tax $\bar{T}$ is levied, the utility maximizing firm is no more able to avoid it than is the profit maximizing firm. This does not, however, prevent the former from making an adjustment. Indeed, since the discretion model has the firm operating in a region that is suboptimal from a profit maximizing standpoint, the firm will choose to revise its strategy in order to maintain a balance between its rewards. Thus, since a lump-sum tax reduces reported profit, the firm will reduce its spending for staff (and thus increase actual and, hence, reported profit) and on emoluments (which also increases reported profit). Output will also be reduced and for the same reason as given above, i.e., optimal output depends on the level of staff selected and as staff is reduced, so is optimal output.

It might be noted that the lump-sum tax is really doing triple duty inasmuch as its effect is identical to that of increasing the minimum

---

[10] As pointed out in the discussion of Midwest Processing Corporation in Chapter 6, these adjustments may involve some complicated lag relations.

[11] In the limit, as S increases and $\partial R/\partial S \to 0$, $\partial^2 R/\partial X \partial S \to 0$ and the output response disappears. That an increase in staff leads to an increase in the optimal value of X can be seen from the slope of the locus $R_x = C_x$ in Figure 1. As S continues to increase, the slope of $R_x = C_x$ increases and eventually becomes vertical.

profit constraint or imposing any sort of fixed charge on the firm. That is, the discretion model predicts that contrary to the traditional theory (but perhaps more in accord with standard business practice), fixed costs do influence the firm's optimum configuration of variable factors.[12] Evidence, albeit of an indirect sort, is gathered on this in Chapter 6.

Although it is not a property that derives from the comparative statics of the model, the fact that a newly installed executive with the assigned objectives of reducing costs can remove staff with ease is an event which is entirely consistent with the managerial discretion model. To explain this only requires that we recognize that the objective of cost reduction is one which implies a low preference for staff. Hence, the manager with a lower preference for staff than his predecessor may typically be able to achieve significant reductions in staff without simultaneously impairing performance. Moreover, when these changes in personnel and objectives occur at the top executive levels (particularly at the level of the president), shrinkage of the entire staff structure may be both attempted and achieved.

3. Application to Public Utilities

Since the types of departures from profit maximizing behavior that are said to exist in public utilities (and other regulated industries) appear to be derivable by a direct application of the proposed model, it may be worthwhile to demonstrate the relevance of the model to this class of firms separately. Alchian and Kessel have discussed this kind of behavior previously [2], but they have not attempted to develop their argument in the context of a model. The behavior they describe follows as a logical consequence of the managerial discretion models developed above.

The rates that a public utility is permitted to charge are set at levels which are intended to allow the utility to cover its costs and earn a fair rate of return [6, p. 1052]. Ordinarily, rates are not adjusted continuously as conditions change but are revised only periodically. In the short run, therefore, a utility may earn above or below normal profit, but this is not a situation that will be long continued; profit will eventually be restored to a fair level by rate adjustments.

Since above-normal profit cannot be long continued and since supernormal profit may invite the early attention of the regulatory commissions, the management of a public utility that has other than profit maximizing objectives has an incentive to hold profits at or below some

---

[12] This point has also been made by Baumol [11, p. 78].

"safe" level. This tendency to absorb profit is further reinforced by the fact that the penalty for inefficient operations is particularly weak among the regulated monopolies. Not only is there a virtual guarantee that rates will be set so as to cover costs and permit the utility to show earnings sufficient to attract new capital but, in addition, the regulatory commissions have not attempted to control costs. Hence, there is a positive reward for absorbing profits without there being an offsetting penalty to discourage this. This situation is said to be responsible for the conditions of large staff and managerial accommodations among the public utilities.

By inserting a maximum (or "safe" level) profit constraint into the model, this kind of behavior can be shown to follow as a direct implication. Thus the objective is to

$$\text{maximize:} \quad U = U[S, M, \pi_R - (\pi_0 + T)]$$

$$\text{subject to:} \quad \text{(i)} \quad \pi_R \geq \pi_0 + T$$

$$\text{(ii)} \quad \pi_R \leq \pi_M$$

where π_M = maximum safe level of profits to report.

For the reasons given previously, the minimum profit constraint is redundant but the maximum profit constraint may be encountered. The problem restated using the method of the Lagrangian multiplier becomes

$$\text{maximize:} \quad L(X, S, M, \lambda)$$

$$= U[S, M, (1 - t)(R - C - S - M) - \pi_0]$$

$$- \lambda[(1 - t)(R - C - S - M) - \pi_M]$$

where $(-\lambda)$ is a Lagrangian multiplier.

Setting the partial derivative of L with respect to X, S, M, and λ equal to zero yields:

$$(9) \qquad \frac{\partial R}{\partial X} = \frac{\partial C}{\partial X}$$

$$(10) \qquad \frac{\partial R}{\partial S} = \frac{-U_1 + (1 - t)(U_3 - \lambda)}{(1 - t)(U_3 - \lambda)}$$

$$(11) \qquad U_2 = (1 - t)(U_3 - \lambda)$$

$$(12) \qquad (1 - t)(R - C - S - M) \leq \pi_M$$

When Equation 12 is satisfied as an inequality, $\lambda = 0$ and Equations 9, 10, and 11 become identical to 6, 7, and 8 obtained previously. When the constraint is encountered, however, λ takes on positive values [76] and the system is further removed from a profit maximization position. This effect can also be seen by perturbating the system with respect to π_M. Assuming that the constraint is binding, it can be shown that $(\partial S/\partial \pi_M)^0 < 0$ and $(\partial M/\partial \pi_M)^0 < 0$ [and $(\partial X/\partial \pi_M)^0 < 0$ due to the connection of optimal output with staff]. Thus, if a binding maximum profit constraint were to be imposed on a firm previously free from such a ceiling, staff and emoluments would be expanded to prevent the firm from violating the constraint and inducing a rate correction. This is precisely the behavior described above.[13]

This type of behavior need not be limited to public utilities, of course. Any firm which, for whatever reason (for example, to discourage antitrust prosecution), finds itself encountering a maximum or "safe" level profit constraint could be expected to exhibit this behavior.

4. Conclusion

Managerial discretion models are designed to study behavior in business firms where competition in the product market is not typically severe. In such circumstances the management will usually enjoy significant discretion in operating the firm. Since the last of the three models developed includes the properties of the first, my summary comments will be confined to it.

Among the properties of the model are

1. The basic behavioral assumption of the model is the same as the basic rationality assumption throughout economics: individuals seek their own self-interest.
2. Under conditions where forces of competition are weak, the model returns implications different from those of the traditional short-run profit maximizing model—implications which it would appear are capable of being tested. These include (a) staff expenditures (or, approximately, general administrative and selling expense)

---

[13] Averch and Johnson have also examined the effect of introducing a safe level profit constraint [6]. Their behavioral assumption, however, is different from mine. They assume that the public utility seeks to maximize *profit* subject to regulatory constraint. As a result, they do not obtain any of the expense responses that I do but find instead that the firm will attempt to inflate its rate base by investing in plant beyond the level called for in traditional theory. By expressing output as a function of labor and capital and making the regulatory constraint a maximum rate of return rather than a maximum profit level, it would appear that this investment response (in addition to the expense responses) can also be obtained from the model above.

may be permitted to absorb significant amounts of resources under conditions of favorable demand but these excesses will tend to disappear in the face of adversity; (b) expenditures for emoluments will tend to vary directly with the business cycle; (c) staff expenditures will increase if an excess profits tax is imposed; (d) the latter will also be true of emoluments; and (e) fixed costs will affect the firm's optimum configuration of variable factors.

3. The model preserves (that is, converges to) the results obtained from the profit maximizing hypothesis under conditions of pure competition.

4. Conditions said to be characteristic of public utilities are obtained by straightforward application of the model.[14]

In addition, the model has the property that it subsumes a rather general set of arguments that have been raised, but seldom tested, against the profit maximization hypothesis. Thus, if the discretion model should be disconfirmed in all but an unimportant subset of circumstances, a large number of arguments contradictory to the classical model would be challenged.

---

[14] In an earlier version of this analysis I argued that "the welfare implications of the model are easily obtained and readily translated into policy proposals" [129, p. 252]. As the discussion in Chapter 9 reveals, however, some of the welfare implications are less obvious than I had believed. They require additional assumptions about the character of the functional relationships than are specified here and may require an analysis of some complicated lagged responses.

I have indicated [129, p. 245, n. 23] that a general preference function that left the relationship between the components unspecified led to the same results as an additive preference function. As shown in Appendices 4-A and 4-B, this is almost, but not completely, accurate. Certain of the cross effects that complicate the analysis of a general preference function are eliminated when the utility function is specified to be additive.

Finally, the comparative statics analysis of the effects of a change in the profits tax rate in [129] fails to mention the offsetting character of the substitution and income effects that are operating (see Appendices 4-A and 4-B for a separation and analysis of these effects).

Corporation Taxes: Income and Substitution Effects

From the utility function $U = U[S, (1 - t)(R - C - S) - \pi_0]$, the following equilibrium relations are obtained:

(1)
$$\frac{\partial U}{\partial X} = U_2(1 - t)\left(\frac{\partial R}{\partial X} - \frac{\partial C}{\partial X}\right) = 0$$

(2)
$$\frac{\partial U}{\partial S} = U_1 + U_2(1 - t)\left(\frac{\partial R}{\partial S} - 1\right) = 0$$

Taking the total differential of these expressions (treating t as a variable and all other parameters as constants) yields

$$U_2(1 - t)\left(\frac{\partial^2 R}{\partial X^2} - \frac{\partial^2 C}{\partial X^2}\right) dX + U_2(1 - t)\frac{\partial^2 R}{\partial X \partial S} dS = 0$$

$$U_2(1 - t)\frac{\partial^2 R}{\partial X \partial S} dX + \left[U_{11} dS + 2U_{12}(1 - t)\left(\frac{\partial R}{\partial S} - 1\right)\right.$$

$$+ U_2(1 - t)\frac{\partial^2 R}{\partial S^2} + U_{22}(1 - t)^2\left(\frac{\partial R}{\partial S} - 1\right)^2\Bigg] dS$$

$$+ \left[U_2(-1)\left(\frac{\partial R}{\partial S} - 1\right) + U_{12}(-1)(R - C - S)\right.$$

$$\left. + U_{22}(1 - t)\left(\frac{\partial R}{\partial S} - 1\right)(-1)(R - C - S)\right] dt = 0$$

Shifting the dt terms to the right-hand side and putting the expression in matrix form, we have

$$\left\|\begin{matrix} U_2(1-t)(R_{xx}-C_{xx}) & U_2(1-t)R_{xs} \\ U_2(1-t)R_{xs} & [U_{11}+2U_{12}(1-t)(R_s-1)+U_2(1-t)R_{ss}+U_{22}(1-t)^2(R_s-1)^2] \end{matrix}\right\|$$

$$\cdot \begin{bmatrix} dX \\ dS \end{bmatrix} = \begin{bmatrix} 0 \\ [U_2+U_{22}(1-t)(R-C-S)](R_s-1)+U_{12}(R-C-S) \end{bmatrix} [dt]$$

Or, representing the matrix by D,

$$D\begin{bmatrix} dX \\ dS \end{bmatrix} = \begin{bmatrix} 0 \\ [U_{12} + U_{22}(1-t)(R_s - 1)](R - C - S) + U_2(R_s - 1) \end{bmatrix} dt$$

Solving for $\partial S/\partial t$ yields

(3) $\left(\dfrac{\partial S}{\partial t}\right)^0$

$$= \frac{U_2(1-t)(R_{xx} - C_{xx})\{[U_{12} + U_{22}(1-t)(R_s - 1)](R - C - S) + U_2(R_s - 1)\}}{|D|}$$

Since $U_2 > 0$, $U_{22} < 0$, and $U_{12} > 0$,[1] the sign of the bracketed expression is ambiguous. It can be shown that this is due to counteracting "income" and net substitution effects. To determine the income effect, differentiate the equilibrium expression (Equations 1 and 2) with respect to the minimum profit constraint π_0:

$$U_2(1-t)(R_{xx} - C_{xx})\frac{\partial X}{\partial \pi_0} + U_2(1-t)R_{xs}\frac{\partial S}{\partial \pi_0} = 0$$

$$U_{11}\frac{\partial S}{\partial \pi_0} + 2U_{12}(1-t)(R_s - 1)\frac{\partial S}{\partial \pi_0}$$

$$+ [U_{22}(1-t)^2(R_s - 1)^2 + U_2(1-t)R_{ss}]\frac{\partial S}{\partial \pi_0}$$

$$+ U_2(1-t)R_{xs}\frac{\partial X}{\partial \pi_0} - U_{22}(1-t)(R_s - 1) - U_{12}(-1) = 0$$

Or, in matrix form,

$$\begin{Vmatrix} U_2(1-t)(R_{xx} - C_{xx}) & U_2(1-t)R_{xs} \\ U_2(1-t)R_{xs} & U_{11} + 2U_{12}(1-t)(R_s - 1) + U_2(1-t)R_{ss} + U_{22}(1-t)^2(R_s - 1)^2 \end{Vmatrix}$$

$$\cdot \begin{bmatrix} \partial X/\partial \pi_0 \\ \partial S/\partial \pi_0 \end{bmatrix} = \begin{bmatrix} 0 \\ U_{12} + U_{22}(1-t)(R_s - 1) \end{bmatrix}$$

Solving for $\partial S/\partial \pi_0$ yields

(4) $\dfrac{\partial S}{\partial \pi_0}\Big|_{t=t_0} = \dfrac{U_2(1-t)(R_{xx} - C_{xx})[U_{12} + U_{22}(1-t)(R_s - 1)]}{|D|}$

---

[1] The signs of U_2 and U_{22} are unambiguously positive and negative, respectively. The sign of U_{12} is assumed to be positive. See the discussion of the "income effect" that follows for a more complete examination of the sign of this cross partial.

Substituting this relation into Equation 3, we obtain

$$(5) \quad \left(\frac{\partial S}{\partial t}\right)^0 = \frac{U_2^2(R_s - 1)(1 - t)(R_{xx} - C_{xx})}{|D|} + (R - C - S)\frac{\partial S}{\partial \pi_0}\Bigg|_{t=t_0}$$

where $(R - C - S)\dfrac{\partial S}{\partial \pi_0}\Bigg|_{t=t_0}$ is the *income effect.*

By inspection of Equation 4, $\dfrac{\partial S}{\partial \pi_0}\Bigg|_{t=t_0}$ will be unambiguously negative if U_{12} is

assumed to be ≥ 0 [since $U_2 > 0$, $(R_{xx} - C_{xx}) < 0$, $U_{22} < 0$, $(R_s - 1) < 0$, and $|D| > 0$]. Recalling our argument that the indifference curves tend to flatten at successively lower levels of profit, and recognizing that the slope of the indifference curve is given by the marginal rate of substitution, we have

$$\text{MRS} = \frac{\partial U/\partial S}{\partial U/\partial \pi}$$

Differentiating this with respect to π we have

$$\frac{\partial}{\partial \pi}(\text{MRS}) = \frac{\dfrac{\partial U}{\partial \pi}\left(\dfrac{\partial^2 U}{\partial S \partial \pi}\right) - \dfrac{\partial U}{\partial S}\left(\dfrac{\partial^2 U}{\partial \pi^2}\right)}{(\partial U/\partial \pi)^2} = \frac{U_2 U_{12} - U_1 U_{22}}{U_2^2}$$

Now $U_2 > 0$, $U_1 > 0$, and $U_{22} < 0$ unambiguously. Thus if it is assumed that $U_{12} \geq 0$, this expression for the change in the marginal rate of substitution with respect to an increase in profits (staff held constant) will be unambiguously positive. In other words, at successively lower values of profit, the marginal rate of substitution will fall, as required. Moreover, if the utility function

$$U = U[S, (1 - t)(R - C - S) - \pi_0]$$

is assumed to be multiplicative, U_{12} will be unambiguously positive, whereas, if it is assumed to be additive, U_{12} will be zero. Thus the assumption that $U_{12} \geq 0$ seems reasonable both from the standpoint of the marginal rate of substitution relations as well as from the specializations of the utility function indicated above. Hence, *the income effect is always negative.*

To eliminate the income effect and thereby isolate the net substitution effect, consider an increase dt in the tax rate t accompanied by a compensating increase in profit $-d\pi_0 = (R - C - S)\,dt$.[2] The corresponding change in

---

[2] The treatment here follows Allen [3, p. 662]. The negative sign is required since $d\pi_0$ without the negative would yield a penalizing rather than a compensating variation.

demand for S is[3]

$$dS = \frac{\partial S}{\partial t}\,dt + \frac{\partial S}{\partial \pi_0}\,d\pi_0$$

But, by assumption, $-d\pi_0 = (R - C - S)\,dt$. Hence,

$$(6) \qquad \frac{dS}{dt} = \frac{\partial S}{\partial t} - (R - C - S)\frac{\partial S}{\partial \pi_0}$$

Substituting the expression for $\partial S/\partial t$ from Equation 5 into Equation 6 reveals that compensated variation in the demand for S is

$$(7) \qquad \frac{dS}{dt} = \frac{U_2^2(R_s - 1)(1 - t)(R_{xx} - C_{xx})}{|D|}$$

The *net substitution effect*, Equation 7, is always positive, since $(R_s - 1) < 0$, $(R_{xx} - C_{xx}) < 0$, and $|D| > 0$.

The combined response of S to an increase in the tax rate t can thus be examined in two parts. Substituting Equation 7 into 5 gives

$$(8) \qquad \left(\frac{\partial S}{\partial t}\right)^0 = \frac{dS}{dt}\bigg|_{U=\bar{U}} + (R - C - S)\frac{dS}{d\pi_0}\bigg|_{t=t_0}$$

The gross substitution effect is the combination of the net substitution effect and the income effect; its sign depends on the relative magnitudes of the individual effects. In general, I expect that the net substitution effect exceeds the income effect so that the gross effect is positive.

Consider, for example, the following additive utility function:

$$U = \alpha_1 S^{\beta_1} + \alpha_2[(1 - t)(R - C - S) - \pi_0]^{\beta_2}$$

where $\alpha_1, \alpha_2 > 0; 0 < \beta_1 < 1; 0 < \beta_2 < 1$. Then

$$(9) \qquad U_2 = \alpha_2\beta_2[(1 - t)(R - C - S) - \pi_0]^{\beta_2 - 1}$$

$$(10) \qquad U_{12} = 0$$

$$(11) \qquad U_{22} = \alpha_2\beta_2(\beta_2 - 1)[(1 - t)(R - C - S) - \pi_0]^{\beta_2 - 2}$$

Whether the gross substitution effect is positive or negative depends on the sign of the expression

$$[U_{12} + U_{22}(1 - t)(R_s - 1)](R - C - S) + U_2(R_s - 1)$$

---

[3] The demand function for S is $S = S(t, \pi_0)$.

in Equation 3. Substituting the relations from 9, 10, and 11 into this expression yields:

$$(12) \quad \alpha_2\beta_2(\beta_2 - 1)[(1 - t)(R - C - S) - \pi_0]^{\beta_2-2}(1 - t)(R_s - 1)(R - C - S)$$
$$+ \alpha_2\beta_2[(1 - t)(R - C - S) - \pi_0]^{\beta_2-1} \gtreqless 0$$

This can be rewritten as

$$(R_s - 1)[\beta_2(1 - t)(R - C - S) - \pi_0] \gtreqless 0$$

If $\pi_0 = 0$, this expression is unambiguously negative, and, hence, the gross substitution effect will be positive. As the firm encounters adversity, however, $(1 - t)(R - C - S)$ will approach π_0 and the inequality becomes less positive and could become negative, in which event the gross substitution effect will be negative.

The onset of adversity, which drives the difference $[(1 - t)(R - C - S) - \pi_0]$ towards zero, has the same type of effect if the utility function is assumed to be multiplicative rather than additive.

The Scope of Qualitative Economics Extended

In his recent article, "The Scope of Qualitative Economics," Lancaster defines qualitative economics as an analysis in which "the algebraic sign of some effect is predicted from the knowledge of the signs, only, of the relevant structural parameters of the system" [77, p. 99]. He finds that this approach to the study of economic systems has not been systematically developed and sets out to remedy this condition by developing a "qualitative calculus" [77, pp. 103–6]. This entails specifying a number of criteria under which the sign matrix will produce qualitative predictions. Thus he develops (1) counting criteria involving the number of zeros in the matrix and the distribution of the signs of the positive and negative elements and (2) criteria involving arrangement. The first of these criteria provide necessary conditions for qualitative solutions, the second assure sufficiency.

After demonstrating the relevance of this approach to a comparison of the Keynesian and classical systems, he goes on to consider what he calls "semi-qualitative" relationships.

> The most typical example of such relationships in economic analysis is that of convexity-concavity or static "stability," which is basic to most traditional analysis of the behavior of the firm and the consumer. As is well known, convexity of a function, for example, a utility index, cannot be given from knowledge of the signs of the second order partial derivatives, but requires quantitative relationships between these derivatives to hold. These relationships will also be relevant to the comparative static properties of the system [77, pp. 111].

He then shows that the knowledge that the matrix of the second partials of the equilibrium relations is positive definite for a true minimum (or negative definite for a true maximum) can be used in determining the response of the system under certain restrictive conditions [77, p. 111]. To obtain further knowledge of the system response, Lancaster requires the use of quantitative information.

It is my contention that this view of qualitative economics neglects what may be an important class of information. Certainly with respect to the present study, this is the case. He fails to consider the possibility that, although the directions of the responses may not be unambiguously determinable from the *signs* of the second partials alone, algebraic solution of the system in terms of its second partials may lead to cancellations which then yield unambiguous results. This is best shown by example.

Consider the staff-emoluments model developed earlier in the chapter. The objective was to

$$\text{maximize:} \quad U = U[S, M, (1 - t)(R - C - S - M) - \pi_0]$$

First-order conditions for an extremum were

(1)
$$\frac{\partial U}{\partial X} = U_3(1 - t)\left(\frac{\partial R}{\partial X} - \frac{\partial C}{\partial X}\right) = 0$$

(2)
$$\frac{\partial U}{\partial S} = U_1 + U_3(1 - t)\left(\frac{\partial R}{\partial S} - 1\right) = 0$$

(3)
$$\frac{\partial U}{\partial M} = U_2 - U_3(1 - t) = 0$$

We want to examine the response of the system to an increase in each of the parameters. Consider, for example, an increase in the profits tax rate t. The effect of this change is found by differentiating each of the equilibrium equations with respect to t, holding each of the other parameters constant but treating all of the unknowns as variable. This yields:

(1')
$$U_3(1 - t)\left(\frac{\partial^2 R}{\partial X^2} - \frac{\partial^2 C}{\partial X^2}\right)\left(\frac{\partial X}{\partial t}\right)^0 + U_3(1 - t)\left(\frac{\partial^2 R}{\partial X \partial S}\right)\left(\frac{\partial S}{\partial t}\right)^0 = 0$$

(2')
$$\left[U_{11} + 2U_{13}\left(\frac{\partial R}{\partial S} - 1\right)(1 - t)\right.$$

$$+ U_{33}(1 - t)^2\left(\frac{\partial R}{\partial S} - 1\right)^2 + U_3(1 - t)\left(\frac{\partial^2 R}{\partial S^2}\right)\left]\left(\frac{\partial S}{\partial t}\right)^0\right.$$

$$+ \left[U_{12} - (1 - t)U_{13} + U_{23}(1 - t)\left(\frac{\partial R}{\partial S} - 1\right)\right.$$

$$- U_{33}(1 - t)^2\left(\frac{\partial R}{\partial S} - 1\right)\left]\left(\frac{\partial M}{\partial t}\right)^0 + U_3(1 - t)\left(\frac{\partial^2 R}{\partial X \partial S}\right)\left(\frac{\partial X}{\partial t}\right)^0\right.$$

$$+ \left[-U_{13}(R - C - S - M) - U_{33}(1 - t)(R - C - S - M)\left(\frac{\partial R}{\partial S} - 1\right)\right.$$

$$\left. - U_3\left(\frac{\partial R}{\partial S} - 1\right)\right] = 0$$

$$(3') \quad \left[U_{12} + U_{23}(1-t)\left(\frac{\partial R}{\partial S} - 1\right) \right.$$

$$\left. - U_{13}(1-t) - U_{33}(1-t)^2 \left(\frac{\partial R}{\partial S} - 1\right) \right]\left(\frac{\partial S}{\partial t}\right)^0$$

$$+ \left[U_{22} - 2U_{23}(1-t) + U_{33}(1-t)^2 \right]\left(\frac{\partial M}{\partial t}\right)^0$$

$$- U_{23}(R - C - S - M) + U_3 + U_{33}(R - C - S - M)(1-t) = 0$$

Putting the system in matrix form we obtain

$$(4) \quad D \begin{bmatrix} \left(\dfrac{\partial X}{\partial t}\right)^0 \\[2ex] \left(\dfrac{\partial S}{\partial t}\right)^0 \\[2ex] \left(\dfrac{\partial M}{\partial t}\right)^0 \end{bmatrix} = \begin{bmatrix} 0 \\[2ex] [U_{13}+U_{33}(1-t)(R_s-1)](R-C-S-M)+U_3(R_s-1) \\[2ex] [U_{23}-U_{33}(1-t)](R-C-S-M)-U_3 \end{bmatrix}$$

where

$$D = \begin{Vmatrix} U_3(1-t)(R_{xx}-C_{xx}) & U_3(1-t)R_{xs} & 0 \\[3ex] U_3(1-t)R_{xs} & \begin{matrix} U_{11}+2U_{13}(R_s-1)(1-t) \\ +U_{33}(1-t)^2(R_s-1)^2 \\ +U_3(1-t)(R_{ss}) \end{matrix} & \begin{matrix} U_{12}-(1-t)U_{13} \\ +U_{23}(1-t)(R_s-1) \\ -U_{33}(1-t)^2(R_s-1) \end{matrix} \\[4ex] 0 & \begin{matrix} U_{12}+U_{23}(1-t)(R_s-1) \\ -U_{13}(1-t) \\ -U_{33}(1-t)^2(R_s-1) \end{matrix} & \begin{matrix} U_{22}-2U_{23}(1-t) \\ +U_{33}(1-t)^2 \end{matrix} \end{Vmatrix}$$

is the matrix of the second partial derivatives of the equilibrium relations. That is,

$$D = \begin{Vmatrix} U_{xx} & U_{xs} & U_{xm} \\ U_{xs} & U_{ss} & U_{sm} \\ U_{xm} & U_{sm} & U_{mm} \end{Vmatrix} = \begin{Vmatrix} - & + & 0 \\ + & - & -? \\ 0 & -? & - \end{Vmatrix}$$

Moreover, the right-hand side of Equation 4 is merely the column vector

$\partial^2 U/\partial Z_i \partial t$, where $Z_i = X, S, M$. The column vector has the signs

$$\begin{bmatrix} 0 \\ ? \\ ? \end{bmatrix}$$

The solution to Equation 4 reduces to

(5)
$$\left(\frac{\partial Z_j}{\partial t}\right)^0 = \frac{-\sum_{i=1}^{3} \frac{\partial^2 U}{\partial Z_i \partial t} D_{ij}}{|D|}$$

Using the sign relations for D and $\partial^2 U/\partial Z_i \partial t$, the following determinantal solution for $(\partial S/\partial t)^0$ is obtained:

$$\left(\frac{\partial S}{\partial t}\right)^0 = -\frac{(-1)^3 D_{12}(0) + (-1)^4 D_{22}(?) + (-1)^5 D_{32}(?)}{|D|}$$

Second-order conditions require that the determinants of the principal minors alternate in sign, beginning with a negative. Thus

$$\left(\frac{\partial S}{\partial t}\right)^0 = (+)[0 + D_{22}(?) - D_{32}(?)] = [0 + (+)(?) - (?)(?)]$$

Since the sign of this expression is uncertain, the response of staff to an increase in the tax rate remains unknown.

Solving the system in terms of the general functional relationships shown in Equation 4, however, substantially removes the ambiguity. Thus, we have

$$D_{22} = U_{xx}U_{mm} = U_{xx}[U_{22} - 2U_{23}(1 - t) + U_{33}(1 - t)^2]$$

$$D_{32} = U_{xx}U_{sm} = U_{xx}[U_{12} - U_{13}(1 - t) + U_{23}(1 - t)(R_s - 1)$$
$$- U_{33}(1 - t)^2(R_s - 1)]$$

$$\frac{\partial^2 U}{\partial S \partial t} = [-U_{13} - U_{33}(1 - t)(R_s - 1)](R - C - S - M) - U_3(R_s - 1)$$

$$\frac{\partial^2 U}{\partial M \partial t} = [U_{33}(1 - t) - U_{23}](R - C - S - M) + U_3$$

Solving for $(\partial S/\partial t)^0$ in terms of these expressions, we have

$$\left(\frac{\partial S}{\partial t}\right)^0 = (+)\{0 + U_{xx}[U_{12} - 2U_{23}(1 - t) + U_{33}(1 - t)^2] \cdot$$

$$\{[-U_{13} - U_{33}(1 - t)](R - C - S - M) - U_3(R_s - 1)\}$$
$$- U_{xx}[U_{12} - U_{13}(1 - t) + U_{23}(1 - t)(R_s - 1) - U_{33}(1 - t)^2(R_s - 1)] \cdot$$
$$\{[U_{33}(1 - t) - U_{23}](R - C - S - M) + U_3\}\}$$

It can be shown that collecting terms in $(R - C - S - M)$ yields identically the expression for $(\partial S/\partial \pi_0)^0$, which permits us to split out the income effect. Thus, we have

$$\left(\frac{\partial S}{\partial t}\right)^0 = (+)\{U_{xx}[U_{22} - 2U_{23}(1 - t) + U_{33}(1 - t)^2][-U_3(R_s - 1)]$$

$$- U_{xx}[U_{12} - U_{13}(1 - t) + U_{23}(1 - t)(R_s - 1) - U_{33}(1 - t)^2(R_s - 1)]U_3$$

$$+ (R - C - S - M)U_{xx}[U_{22} - 2U_{23}(1 - t) + U_{33}(1 - t)^2] \cdot$$
$$[-U_{13} - U_{33}(1 - t)(R_s - 1)]$$

$$- (R - C - S - M)U_{xx}[U_{12} - U_{13}(1 - t) + U_{23}(1 - t)(R_s - 1)$$
$$- U_{33}(1 - t)^2(R_s - 1)][-U_{23} + U_{33}]\}$$

Without performing cancellations, however, assigning sign relations to these expressions in which the income and net substitution effects have been separated fails to yield unambiguous results; it is not enough merely to separate out the income from the net substitution effect. After performing the appropriate cancellations, however, we obtain

$$\left(\frac{\partial S}{\partial t}\right)^0 = (+)\{+U_{xx}[-U_{22}U_3(R_s - 1) + U_{23}(1 - t)U_3(R_s - 1)$$

$$- U_{12}U_3 + U_{13}(1 - t)U_3]$$

$$+ (R - C - S - M)U_{xx}[-U_{22}U_{13} + U_{23}(1 - t)U_{13} - U_{22}U_{33}(1 - t)(R_s - 1)$$

$$+ U_{12}U_{23}^2(1 - t)(R_s - 1) - U_{12}U_{33}(1 - t)]\}$$

The first term in this expression corresponds to the net substitution effect and the second term is the income effect. Thus we can write

$$\frac{\partial S}{\partial t}\bigg|_{U = \bar{U}} = (+)\{U_{xx}[-U_{22}U_3(R_s - 1) + U_{23}(1 - t)U_3(R_s - 1)$$

$$- U_{12}U_3 + U_{13}(1 - t)U_3]\}$$

and

$$(R - C - S - M)\frac{\partial S}{\partial \pi_0}\bigg|_{t = t_0} = (+)\{U_{xx}[-U_{22}U_{13} + U_{23}(1 - t)U_{13}$$

$$- U_{22}U_{33}(1 - t)(R_s - 1) + U_{12}U_{23} + U_{23}^2(1 - t)(R_s - 1) - U_{12}U_{33}(1 - t)]\}$$

Assuming $U_{ij} > 0$ for $i \neq j$ (and of course $U_i > 0$, $U_{ii} > 0$, and $(R_s - 1) < 0$),[1] we find that there is only one term in each of these expressions which leaves the sign of each unknown. If, however, we assume that $U_{ij} = 0$ for $i \neq j$ (as would

---

[1] See Appendix 4-A for a rationale for the relation $U_{ij} > 0$, for $i \neq j$.

be true, for example, if the utility function were additive in each of its components), the net substitution effect is unambiguously negative and the income effect is unambiguously positive. Without performing the cancellations, however, the signs of both these expressions would be uncertain.

Moreover, it seems reasonable to assert that

$$U_{22}U_3(R_s - 1) - U_3(R_s - 1) + U_{12}U_3 > U_{13}(1 - t)U_3$$

where each term on both sides of the inequality is positive. Under these conditions, the net substitution effect is positive even if $U_{ij} > 0$ for $i \neq j$.[2] Similarly, if

$$-U_{22}U_{13} + U_{23}(1 - t)U_{13} - U_{22}U_{33}(1 - t)(R_s - 1) + U_{12}U_{23} - U_{12}U_{33}(1 - t)$$
$$> -U_{23}^2(1 - t)(R_s - 1)$$

where all the terms on both sides of this inequality are also positive, the income effect is negative even if $U_{ij} > 0$ for $i \neq j$.

The gross substitution effect of course depends on the relative magnitude of the net substitution and income effects. As the argument in Appendix 4–A indicated, the gross substitution effect will normally be positive, but it can be negative.

To summarize, the failure of the signed relations to produce an unambiguous directional response of the decision variables to a change in a parameter does not mean that purely qualitative (or quasi-qualitative) relations are unable to permit such a determination. As shown above, and as is true for all of the responses in the staff-emoluments model,[3] a detailed examination of the functional relations often permits a cancellation of terms so that the remaining terms lead to a nearly certain result.[4]

---

[2] Assuming that staff and profits are substitutes rather than complements, which has clearly been the burden of the argument, the net substitution effect is necessarily positive.

[3] Only the tax responses depend on the contingent income-substitution argument of Appendix 4-A. All, however, have to be solved from their functional rather than sign relationships in order to discover the direction of the response.

[4] Professor Simon informs me that he has encountered this same phenomenon in his analysis of the comparative statics properties of other systems. I will try to generalize this approach at a later time since, as he suggests, it may have general application.

CHAPTER 5

A Morphology of Models of the Business Firm: II, Entrepreneurial Models and Sales Maximization Hypothesis

Although the managerial discretion models include profit maximization as a limiting case, they are primarily designed to study business behavior in conditions where competition in the product market is not severe and where the management is in effective control of the firm. Although the second of these conditions may frequently be satisfied, the first may be less often fulfilled. Where it is not, but instead competitors are numerous and entry is easy, the analysis can be simplified by using the profit maximization assumption. Models which assume that the firm is operated as *if* to maximize profit will be referred to as *entrepreneurial models*. Nonpecuniary satisfactions are either nonexistent, unimportant, or incapable of being realized.

Two versions of the entrepreneurial model are examined. The first is the usual or short-run profit maximizing model. It assumes that the planning horizon extends over only a single period. The second is the long-run construction. In this case, the planning horizon is assumed to extend over a number of periods. Whereas the short-period analysis merely entails reproducing an already existing model, the multi-period analysis involves constructing a model and developing implications which, although probably well-known, do not appear to be generally available in the literature.

72

In addition to the entrepreneurial models, Baumol's sales maximization hypothesis is also investigated. Of interest is the way he motivates the analysis as well as the implications he obtains.

1. Entrepreneurial Models[1]

1.1. Short-Run Profit Maximization.
The short-run profit maximization model assumes that the entire objective of the firm is to maximize profit and that this is done by equating current period marginal costs to benefits. Thus, the management is assumed to operate the firm so as to

$$\text{maximize:} \quad \pi = (1 - t)(R - C - S - \bar{T})$$

First-order conditions for a maximum are found by setting partial derivatives of π with respect to X and S equal to zero. This yields

$$(1) \qquad \frac{\partial R}{\partial X} = \frac{\partial C}{\partial X}$$

$$(2) \qquad \frac{\partial R}{\partial S} = 1$$

That is, output is chosen so that marginal gross revenue is equal to

---

[1] These entrepreneurial models are what I have previously designated as the *classical* theory of the firm. Actually, they involve an elaboration of the standard profit maximizing model as applied to the analysis of monopoly behavior. The elaboration results from adding a staff term so that $P = P(X, S)$, $\partial P/\partial X < 0$ and $\partial P/\partial S > 0$, to the conventional monopoly construction, (where $P = P(X)$, $\partial P/\partial X < 0$). The argument for neglecting the staff term in the standard treatment of the theory of the firm is that the production and staff decisions are symmetrical [120, p. 251]. Hence, to include both yields no insights that are not obtained by looking at the output decision alone. That this is so is readily seen by inspection of the short-run profit maximization model below. However, where the staff planning horizon exceeds the production planning horizon, this symmetry disappears and the justification for absorbing the staff variable in the output variable vanishes. The necessity for introducing the two terms separately is shown in the long-period or discounted profit maximization model.

The entrepreneurial models proposed thus preserve the profit maximization assumption of classical monopoly theory, but extend the analysis to include staff. This elaboration should not be interpreted as one that converts the analysis into the monopolistic competition case (with its free entry and excess capacity properties). For a discussion of the entry question in a selling expense context, see my discussion in [128].

the marginal costs of production, and staff is selected so that the marginal value product of staff is equal to its marginal cost. This position corresponds with the point K in Figures 1 and 2 of Chapter 4.

The comparative statics properties of the model are found by the same procedures used for examining the models in the previous chapter. The sign matrix of the second partials of π is

$$D = \left\| \begin{matrix} - & + \\ + & - \end{matrix} \right\|$$

The signs of the values $\partial^2 \pi / \partial Z_i \partial \alpha_k$ for $Z_i = X$, S and $\alpha_k = E, t, \bar{T}$ are

$$\left\| \frac{\partial^2 \pi}{\partial Z_i \partial \alpha_k} \right\| = \begin{matrix} & E & t & \bar{T} \\ X & + & 0 & 0 \\ S & + & 0 & 0 \end{matrix}$$

Comparative statics responses can be obtained from the signs of the partial derivatives of the equilibrium relations as displayed above alone. They are shown in Table 1.

Unlike the final version of the managerial model (and of the first or "staff" version of it as well), the firm that maximizes short-run profit is entirely unresponsive to changes in the profits tax rate and to a lump-sum tax. Furthermore, it does not absorb any of its profit as emoluments. Finally, the magnitude of its responses to a change in the condition of the environment will, *ceteris paribus*, normally be smaller than in the utility maximizing firm (see Section 2 in Chapter 6). The absence of slack in its operations as contrasted with the calculated accumulation (and de-cumulation) of slack by the utility maximizing firm is responsible for these quantitative differences. Thus the differences between this, the traditional theory of the firm construction, and the discretion model are numerous and presumably capable of being tested.

TABLE 1. COMPARATIVE STATICS RESPONSES FOR THE SHORT-RUN
PROFIT MAXIMIZATION MODEL

	Parameter		
	E	t	$\bar{T}$
X^0	+	0	0
Variable			
S^0	+	0	0

1.2. Long-Run Profit Maximization. A more responsive entrepreneurial model can be obtained by devising a multi-period, discounted
version of the profit maximization hypothesis. The variables are subscripted by time periods by i, where $i = 1, 2, \ldots, n$, and where n is the
planning horizon. Letting r be the discount rate, profits in year i will
be discounted by $1/(1 + r)^{i-1}$. Let this be represented by α^{i-1}.

It is assumed that production decisions in period k affect costs in no
other period or, if there are effects, that these are offsetting. However,
staff expenditures in period k are assumed to have a positive influence
on future period revenues over the entire planning horizon. Indeed, the
length of the "period" can be defined as the interval beyond which current production decisions have no effect, and the length of the planning
horizon as the number of such periods for which current staff expenditures have a positive effect.[2]

Letting π represent the discounted value of profits, the objective is to

$$\text{maximize:} \quad \pi = \sum_{i=1}^{n} (1 - t)(R_i - C_i - S_i - \bar{T}_i)\alpha^{i-1}$$

First-order conditions for a maximum are obtained by setting the
partial derivatives of π with respect to X_1 and S_1 equal to zero. Thus we
have

$$(3) \qquad \frac{\partial R_1}{\partial X_1} = \frac{\partial C_1}{\partial X_1}$$

$$(4) \qquad \frac{\partial R_1}{\partial S_1} = 1 - \sum_{i=2}^{n} \frac{\partial R_i}{\partial S_1} \alpha^{i-1}$$

Inspection of Equation 3 reveals that the firm chooses that value
of output for which the marginal gross revenue is equal to the marginal
costs of production. Equation 4, however, shows that the current

---

[2] It might be noted that these same assumptions can be introduced into the
utility functions examined previously. All this entails is substituting

$$[\sum_{i=1}^{n} (1 - t)(R_i - C_i - S_i - \bar{T}_i) - \pi_0]$$

for the

$$[(1 - t)(R - C - S - \bar{T}) - \pi_0]$$

term that appears in the utility functions presently. Since none of the qualitative
properties of the managerial models would be affected by such a substitution, the
analysis is made simpler by using a single-period construction.

marginal value product of staff is less than its current marginal cost.[3]
These equilibrium conditions are thus similar to those obtained from
the discretion model.

The sign matrix of the second partials of the equilibrium relations is

$$D = \begin{Vmatrix} - & + \\ + & - \end{Vmatrix}$$

Since the effects of levying the profits tax for a period less than the
planning horizon are different from those when the tax covers the
entire horizon, the profits tax is split into "temporary" (designated by
tax rate t') and "permanent" (designated by tax rate t'') types. The
signs of the values $\partial^2\pi/\partial Z_i\partial\alpha_k$ for $Z_i = X_1$, S_1 and $\alpha_k = E, t', t'', \bar{T}$ are

$$\begin{Vmatrix} \dfrac{\partial^2\pi}{\partial Z_i\partial\alpha_k} \end{Vmatrix} = \begin{array}{c c c c c} & E & t' & t'' & \bar{T} \\ X_1 & + & 0 & 0 & 0 \\ S_1 & + & + & 0 & 0 \end{array}$$

The comparative statics responses are obtained directly from the
sign relationships alone (Table 2).

The responses to a change in the conditions of the environment E
are as expected. More interesting are the tax effects. A temporary
increase in the profits tax rate encourages additional expenditures on
staff (and, hence, output also increases). Thus, although current
profits are reduced as a result, these are high tax profits; and since the
spending on staff now produces larger revenues and profits in the post-
tax period, a change in spending that reduces current but favors future
profits occurs. Of course the longer the duration of the change in the

TABLE 2. COMPARATIVE STATICS RESPONSES FOR THE DISCOUNTED
PROFIT MAXIMIZING MODEL

| | | Parameter | | | |
		E	t'	t''	$\bar{T}$
Variable	X_1^0	+	+	0	0
	S_1^0	+	+	0	0

---

[3] Over the entire horizon, however, the discounted value of the marginal value
product of staff equals its marginal cost.

profits tax, the less the response. Finally, when the duration equals or exceeds the length of the planning horizon, the tax change is treated as "permanent" and, as seen from the response to t'', no change whatsoever occurs in staff (or output).

The lump-sum tax $\bar{T}$ produces no change in the discounted profit maximizing firm's choice of variable factors. Again there is no provision for absorbing any fraction of actual profit as emoluments.

Additional responses can be extracted from this multi-period model if a minimum current period profit constraint is introduced. That is, it is assumed that the firm is operated so as to

$$\text{maximize:} \quad \pi = \sum_{i=1}^{n} (1 - t)(R_i - C_i - S_i - \bar{T}_i)\alpha^{i-1}$$

$$\text{subject to:} \quad (1 - t)\pi_1 \geq \pi_0$$

This can be set up as a Lagrangian. The expression becomes

$$\text{maximize:} \quad L(X_1, S_1, \lambda) = \sum_{i=1}^{n} (1 - t)(R_i - C_i - S_i - \bar{T}_i)\alpha^{i-1}$$

$$+ \lambda[(1 - t)(R_1 - C_1 - S_1 - \bar{T}_1) - \pi_0]$$

First-order conditions for a maximum are obtained by setting partial derivatives of L with respect to X_1, S_1, and λ equal to zero. These yield

$$(5) \qquad \frac{\partial R_1}{\partial X_1} = \frac{\partial C_1}{\partial X_1}$$

$$(6) \qquad \frac{\partial R_1}{\partial S_1} = 1 - \frac{1}{1 + \lambda} \sum_{i=2}^{n} \frac{\partial R_i}{\partial S_1} \alpha^{i-1}$$

$$(7) \qquad (1 - t)(R_1 - C_1 - S_1 - \bar{T}_1) \geq \pi_0$$

If the constraint is binding, Equation 7 is satisfied as an equality and, from the Kuhn-Tucker theorem [76], $\lambda > 0$. If the constraint is not binding and the inequality obtains, $\lambda = 0$. The latter case (that is, when the constraint is not binding and $\lambda = 0$) yields precisely the equilibrium and comparative statics properties obtained before the constraint was introduced into the analysis. When the constraint is binding and λ exceeds zero, however, a new class of relations develop. Thus, as λ increases, the current marginal value product of staff is moved in the direction of restoring an equality with its current marginal cost. That is, in order to satisfy the current period minimum profit constraint, future period profits are foregone and the discounted marginal value product of staff exceeds its marginal cost.

The sign matrix of the bordered Hessian of the second partials is

$$
D = \begin{Vmatrix} - & + & 0 \\ + & - & - \\ 0 & - & 0 \end{Vmatrix}
$$

The signs of the values of $\partial^2 L / \partial Z_i \partial \alpha_k$ for $Z_i = X_1$, S_1, λ and $\alpha_k = E$, t', t'', $\bar{T}$ are

$$
\begin{Vmatrix} \dfrac{\partial^2 L}{\partial Z_i \partial \alpha_k} \end{Vmatrix} =
\begin{array}{c c c c c}
 & E & t' & t'' & \bar{T} \\
X_1 & + & 0 & 0 & 0 \\
S_1 & + & + & 0 & 0 \\
\lambda & + & - & - & - \\
\end{array}
$$

Comparative statics responses for the condition when the constraint is binding are given in Table 3.

Again the response to changes in the condition of the environment are in the expected directions, and the interesting responses are those due to changes in the tax rates. Whether the profits tax rate is "temporary" or "permanent," the firm responds by cutting back on staff expenditures (and, hence, also on output). That staff is reduced in response to a "temporary" increase in the profits tax rate reverses the result obtained for the case where the constraint is not binding. The reason is that, being pressed against its minimum acceptable level profit constraint, the additional tax requires the firm to forego future benefits in order to realize an "acceptable level" of current profits by reducing those current expenditures that contribute to future profits; namely, staff. In the case

TABLE 3. COMPARATIVE STATICS RESPONSES FOR THE DISCOUNTED
PROFIT MAXIMIZING MODEL WHEN CONSTRAINT IS BINDING

| | | Parameter | | | |
		E	t'	t''	$\bar{T}$
Variable	X_1^0	+	−	−	−
	S_1^0	+	−	−	−

previously examined, where the constraint was not binding, staff expenditures were increased rather than reduced in response to a "temporary" change in the profits tax rate.

A "permanent" change in the profits tax rate, given that the constraint is binding, also requires a reduction in the expenditures for staff, and for the same reasons. This change contrasts with the zero response obtained for the case when the constraint was not binding.

Finally, in response to a levy of a lump-sum tax $\bar{T}$, the firm cuts back on both staff and output, again with the objective of realizing higher current profits—albeit at the expense of future profits.

2. Revenue Maximization Subject to a Minimum Profit Constraint

Baumol asserts that the objective of many large firms is to maximize sales subject to the condition that profits reach some acceptable level. Although he characterizes the evidence for this position as impressionistic, his confidence in it is quite strong:

> Surely it is common experience that, when one asks an executive, "How's business?", he will answer that his *sales* have been increasing (or decreasing), and talk about his profit only as an afterthought, if at all ....
>
> Nor is this failure to emphasize profits a pure rationalization or a mere matter of careless phrasing. Almost every time I have come across a case of conflict between profits and sales the businessmen with whom I worked left little doubt as to where their hearts lay .... A program which explicitly proposes any cut in sales volume, whatever the profit considerations, is likely to meet a cold reception [11, pp. 47–48].

Under this hypothesis, the firm is operated so as to

$$\text{maximize:} \quad R$$

$$\text{subject to:} \quad \pi = \pi_0$$

where $\pi = (1 - t)(R - C - S - \bar{T})$

Setting up the Lagrangian, we obtain

$$L(X, S, \lambda) = R + \lambda[(1 - t)(R - C - S - \bar{T}) - \pi_0]$$

First-order conditions for a maximum are obtained by setting the partial derivatives of L with respect to X, S, and λ equal to zero.

(8) $\dfrac{\partial R}{\partial X} = \dfrac{(1 - t)\lambda}{1 + (1 - t)\lambda} \dfrac{\partial C}{\partial X}$ and $\dfrac{\partial R}{\partial X} < \dfrac{\partial C}{\partial X}$ since $\lambda > 0$

(9) $\dfrac{\partial R}{\partial S} = \dfrac{(1 - t)\lambda}{1 + (1 - t)\lambda}$ and $\dfrac{\partial R}{\partial S} < 1$ since $\lambda > 0$

(10) $(1 - t)(R - C - S - \bar{T}) = \pi_0$

Equation 8 reveals that the output decision is no longer made so as to equate the marginal gross revenue with the marginal costs of production, but instead the firm operates in the region where marginal gross revenue is less than the marginal costs of production. Likewise, the firm chooses staff (actually, Baumol considers only advertising) so that the marginal value product of staff is less than its marginal cost. Whereas in the discretion model $R_s/1$ is less that R_x/C_x, in the sales maximizing organization $R_s/1$ is equal to R_x/C_x. That is, in the sales maximizing firm, the managers have no greater preference for staff than for production. Additional laborers and additional staff expenditures are equally valued. Indeed, they are not only indifferent between them, the management is neutral towards each. The objective is merely to choose that composition of variable factors that most contributes to sales. Thus, instead of expanding the operations of the firm in a manner that favors expenditures on staff (as occurs in the managerial discretion models), the entire scale of the enterprise is expanded generally and without bias towards staff.

The comparative statics properties of this model are again obtained in the same manner as before. The sign matrix of the bordered Hessian is

$$D = \begin{Vmatrix} - & + & - \\ + & - & - \\ - & - & 0 \end{Vmatrix}$$

TABLE 4. COMPARATIVE STATICS RESPONSES FOR THE REVENUE MAXIMIZATION MODEL

		Parameter		
		E	t	$\bar{T}$
Variable	X^0	+	−	−
	S^0	+	−	−

The signs of the values of $\partial^2 L/\partial Z_i \partial \alpha_k$ for $Z_i = X, S, \lambda$ and $\alpha_k = E, t, \bar{T}$ are

$$
\left\| \frac{\partial^2 L}{\partial Z_i \partial \alpha_k} \right\| =
\begin{array}{cccc}
 & E & t & \bar{T} \\
X & + & + & 0 \\
S & + & + & 0 \\
\lambda & + & - & -
\end{array}
$$

Comparative statics responses for this model cannot all be determined by the signs of the partial derivatives of the equilibrium relations as displayed above alone. Rather, some require analysis of the sort described in the Appendix 4-B. The responses are shown in Table 4.

The basic qualitative difference between this model and preceding models is that an increase in the profits tax rate unfailingly causes the firm to reduce staff and output. The reason, of course, is that the minimum profit constraint is assumed to be *always* binding so that any increase in taxes requires the firm to forego revenues and move its decision variables toward a profit maximizing position—independent of the condition of the environment. Again, of course, there are no emoluments responses, no provision having been made for them in this model.

3. Conclusions

The purpose of this chapter has been to consider the motivational assumptions and develop the implications of three alternatives to the discretion models of Chapter 4. Two of these models, the short-run profit maximizing model and Baumol's maximization hypothesis, have been available in the literature for some time. The short-run profit maximizing model has been the basic theory of the firm construction at least since Cournot [37] and its properties are well-known. The sales maximization hypothesis is of more recent vintage. Although its profits tax implications have been previously neglected, my treatment of this model has essentially involved reproducing properties already known to exist.

The multi-period version of the profit maximization hypothesis that was examined does not appear to be generally available in the literature. Hence, this construction, particularly when extended to include a minimum profit constraint, is somewhat new and yields some interesting results.

In addition to the comparative statics responses explicitly examined in this and the preceding chapter, the effects of a sales tax of both the specific and ad valorem variety have been investigated. All of the models yield the same qualitative responses: each predicts that staff and output will be reduced in response to a levy of either of these types of taxes. Thus, the main theorems of the profit maximizing model (of either the single- or multi-period variety) with respect to shifts in demand and the application of a sales tax are preserved by the proposed utility maximizing model. Indeed, since there is little dispute concerning the directions of adjustment of these effects, it would be distressing to have the results go differently. However, when it comes to matters where the qualitative implications of the profit maximizing model have been suspect, namely the effects of a profits tax and a lump-sum tax, the managerial discretion models register responses that contradict the classical theory. Hence there would appear to be genuine grounds for discriminating between these two hypotheses on either of these tax dimensions.

Actually, this conclusion requires qualification because of the greater range of responses displayed by the multi-period than by the single-period profit maximizing model. With respect to the short-run model, the firm is unresponsive to either a change in the profits tax or a lump-sum tax, whereas the discretion models that include a staff component predict that staff and output adjustments will occur in response to both of these types of taxes.

The multi-period profit maximizing model was evaluated in two parts. First, in the absence of a minimum profit constraint (or, equivalently, in the presence of a minimum profit constraint that is not binding), the multi-period profit maximizing model predicts that the firm will respond to a change in the profits tax rate when the tax is of shorter duration than the planning horizon. Staff and output will both be increased in response to an increase in such a "temporary" tax. A "permanent" change in the profits tax rate gives rise to no change, however, and the levy of a lump-sum tax likewise leaves the firm's optimal combination of variable factors unaffected. The managerial discretion models that include a staff component predict that staff and output will increase in response to both a "temporary" and a "permanent" change in the profits tax rate,[4] while a lump-sum tax will cause staff and output to be reduced. These differences are potentially testable.

Should the discounted profit maximizing firm encounter its minimum profit constraint and the utility maximizing firm have difficulty satisfy-

---

[4] As pointed out in the derivation of these results, they require the stipulation that profits exceed minimum profits demanded by a reasonable margin (see Appendix 4-A).

ing its minimum profit constraint, qualitative responses in staff and output to both "temporary" and "permanent" profits taxes as well as to lump-sum tax become indistinguishable.[5] Both classes of models predict that staff and output will be reduced in response to an increase in a profits tax of either type, and a lump-sum tax causes similar adjustments. However, with the exception of serious recession periods (when the difficulty of achieving profit goals may be quite general), these responses are possibly of more academic than practical interest. Hence, the differences indicated above, when the profit constraint is not binding, are of more fundamental importance.

A basic difference between the managerial discretion models and the entrepreneurial models of both types that has not yet been mentioned is the emoluments term that appears in two of the discretion models but has no place in the profit maximizing construction. Evidence that firms expand expenditures on emoluments under favorable environmental conditions or in response to an increase in the profits tax rate would thus support the insertion of the emoluments term into the firm's utility function.

In addition to tests based on comparative statics properties, tests of two other kinds are available. The first of these involves introducing quantitative considerations. That is, although the direction of the response under the alternative hypotheses may be the same, there may be grounds for discriminating between the theories on the basis of differences in their gross quantitative implications. *Ceteris paribus*, the utility maximizing firm will generally undergo larger adjustments in response to changes in demand than will the profit maximizing organization, and these will tend to be concentrated in staff and emoluments. As indicated earlier, these differences are due to the calculated accumulation (and hence de-cumulation) of staff and emoluments in the former that are not present in the latter. Evidence on this question is developed in Chapter 6.

The second type of test available is studies of *particular behavior*. Thus, whereas the proposed theory implies that differences in competition and differences in tastes will have a significant impact on the internal organization of the firm and on the amounts of resources expended for activities that enhance managerial satisfactions, the classical theory implies that tastes are unimportant and that the only effect of reducing

---

[5] In these circumstances, utility maximizing firms will probably experience income effects that more than offset the net substitution effect (see Appendix 4-A), in which case the gross substitution effect becomes negative.

competition is to move the firm's decision variables towards a monopoly position of greater profit. More precisely, the former leads to the proposition that expenses for which a positive preference has been indicated will vary directly with the size of the "opportunity set" (essentially the condition of competition in the product market and, possibly, the extent of stockholder concentration) and the "tastes" of the management for such satisfactions, while the latter predicts that expenses will be responsive only to profit considerations.

I designate tests of this type as tests of particular behavior because they involve extracting implications from the assumptions of the alternative theories additional to the implications for *general behavior* that are obtained from the analysis of equilibrium and comparative statics. They are expressly concerned with testing the proposition that differences in competition in the product market and differences in tastes between managements have a systematic influence on the way in which resources are distributed within the organization. Tests of this sort are reported in Chapter 7.

With minor modifications, the discussion above also applies to the sales maximization hypothesis. Thus, adjustments to a shift in demand will tend to be uniform throughout the sales maximizing firm, whereas they will be more concentrated in staff and emoluments in the utility maximizing firm. Similarly, although the sales maximizing firm will operate at a larger scale than a comparable profit maximizing firm, this is the only way in which the management will absorb profit under this hypothesis. Any other type of activity designed to enhance the satisfaction of managers that impairs profit will simultaneously impair sales. Hence, the management is essentially subject to the same restrictions with respect to discretionary expenditures under both the sales and the profit maximizing hypotheses. Finally, a discrimination between the utility and sales maximizing models on the basis of their profits tax implications is possible, since here the models imply opposite adjustments.

CHAPTER 6

The Evidence from the Field Studies

"The study of extreme instances often provides important leads to the essentials of the situation" [16, p. 5]. This observation summarizes the two main characteristics of the field studies reported in this chapter. First, the field studies are concerned with the behavior of the business firm under reasonably extreme conditions of adversity. Second, the studies lead to some tentative propositions about the importance of expense preference behavior in the operations of the business firm. It should be emphasized, however, that as with most leads, the evidence is suggestive rather than definitive.

The advantage of selecting extreme instances as a basis for deriving tentative propositions about the characteristic behavior of an organism are examined in Section 1. A definition of what constituted adversity in the firms studied and a model for evaluating the responses observed are developed in Section 2.

The intensive interview has some distinct advantages for studying responses to adversity that are unavailable in the ordinary survey. It provides an opportunity for obtaining insights into the ways in which the firm *perceives* its problems, a description of the *processes* it employs in responding to them, and details of the *magnitudes* involved. But it also suffers from the disadvantage that being a study in small numbers, problems of generalization arise. It was believed that since details on the issue of expense preference behavior are somewhat sparse,[1] while surveys dealing with the question at a general level are available elsewhere, the advantages of the intensive interview outweighed the disadvantages. Field study observations on three business firms that had been subjected to adversity are reported in Sections 3, 4, and 5.[2] Some references to the survey literature appear in Section 6.

Rough indications of the effects of a lump-sum tax were obtained as a part of the studies of adversity, and they are discussed in Section 7.

1. On the Use of Extreme Instances

Archibald has observed that there are two problems that complicate the testing of the theory of the firm:

> First, how is any theory which is purely static to be tested at all? The hypothesis, strictly interpreted, says that adjustments take place with zero time-lag, which we know is false. How "unstrictly" can we interpret it, and still have a refutable hypothesis? Second, there is the problem of the ubiquitous *ceteris paribus* clause. If the "other things" are not specified in advance, there is an alibi for any refutation [4, p. 61].

This is a rather strong indictment. Moreover, it is a position for which there is substantial sympathy. Grunberg, for example, has expressed almost identical apprehensions [58]. It is the purpose of this section to show how the extreme instance can be used to alleviate these difficulties.

1.1. Ceteris Paribus and the Extreme Instance. Recourse to the extreme instance is of particular importance for studying phenomena that cannot be easily observed under controlled conditions. In these circumstances it is often difficult to assign causality in any precise way, since a number of influences may be simultaneously impinging on the organism.

---

[1] One of the reasons such details are lacking is that the data are hard to come by. This difficulty of obtaining data meant that the field studies had to be tailored to the firms individually. Although this complicated comparisons between firms, it had the unanticipated advantage of leading to insights on a wider range of issues than was planned when the interviews were originally set up.

[2] Efforts to include a fourth firm were hindered by the reluctance of the management to release details of its operations. Although what data there were appear to be consistent with the other studies, they produce no insights not already available from the others.

Although the impossibility of conducting controlled experiments complicates the problem of analysis, it need not render it hopeless. Thus, even if "other effects" cannot be entirely removed, it may be sufficient that they be made "small." And since what is "small" is typically a relative rather than an absolute question, the extreme instance may provide a way to achieve this result. That is, by examining only those observations provided by nature in which major shifts occur along the dimension of interest, while other variables are changing only moderately, observations very nearly as valuable as those produced by controlled experimentation may obtain. In short, although the *cetera* are never *paria*, it may be possible to treat them as if they were by restricting the analysis to observations of the extreme instance variety.

If our tools for analysis were very sharp, individual effects could be separated out whatever the mix of changes. Essentially it has been the objective of econometrics to provide the tools to satisfy this need. Simultaneous equations models have been developed precisely for this purpose. But the estimation of parameters is dependent on sufficient variation in the variables, and the necessity of collecting accurate data for the entire system often goes unsatisfied. Combined with misspecification of the model, many such analyses come to naught.

The economist, therefore, is interested in the extreme instance as a way of avoiding the problems encountered when the system is simultaneously subject to a variety of influences. He neither needs to specify the entire system nor collect data on all of its parts if the phenomenon of interest is of overriding importance. Without risking serious confounding, he may be able to rely on the extreme instance to provide him with a nearly pure situation to study.[3]

The advantage of the extreme instance should thus be clear. A problem of interpretation, however, remains. If the extreme instance is to be used as a basis for generalizing, care must be taken to assure that the

---

[3] For example, Friedman has argued that the wartime periods provide a particularly appropriate interval for testing Keynesian versus Classical income determination theories [49]. Moreover, in attempting to establish the effect of changing the maturity of the debt on velocity, he selected not a "representative" but a very special period to study. Implicit in the elimination of the bond support program following the Federal Reserve-Treasury accord in 1951 was what Friedman called a "drastic change" in the effective maturity of government bonds [51, p. 61 and n. 5 pp. 107–8]. Scott has also used this same case to determine the effects of altering maturity of the debt in his study of debt management [105]. For the study of inflation, Bresciani-Turroni [24] and Cagan [28] have both taken advantage of the extreme instance by selecting hyperinflation as a means of obtaining insight into the dynamics of inflation.

behavior observed accurately reflects the properties of the system and is not pathological. For the economist this means: Did the response observed differ only in amount but not in kind from that which would be produced by reducing the intensity of the stimulus? In general, as long as (1) the system responds in a systematic and controlled fashion rather than in an erratic and disorganized manner and (2) the actions were taken as a result of deliberation rather than spontaneously without calculated intent, the stress created by the extreme instance can be assumed to be producing a characteristic response. Essentially this is a question of judgment. Prior knowledge of what constitutes rational behavior and knowledge of the decision process leading up to the events observed can be of assistance in making the judgment.

By definition, extreme instances are exceptional circumstances. Hence, large numbers of observations on the phenomena in question may not be easily available. The question of generalizing from small numbers of observations thus arises. Aside from the question of thresholds, this would not appear to be serious as long as (1) the behavior under study is critical to the specie (e.g., related to its continuing survival), (2) the response observed is nonpathological, and (3) the precision required is not great. Additional observations would permit closer definition of the range of responses to expect and the effect of initial conditions to be evaluated. However, these are unlikely to influence the overall estimate of behavior as long as the three conditions given above are satisfied.

The question of sampling remains. As is well-known, in order to have statistical confidence in generalizing from sample results to the population, a random sampling plan is required in which each member of the population, X_i, has a known probability, p_i, of selection. Under stratified sampling procedures where the strata are of equal size, p_i will vary inversely with the sampling cost and directly with the variability of the stratum to which the ith member of the population belongs [30, pp. 75–76].

For small samples where only crude inferences are intended, purposive rather than random samples may frequently have advantages [30, p. 7]. Nonetheless, the criteria for taking observations generally parallel those indicated above. Thus, the study of extreme instances is essentially an application of the variability criterion. Within the subset of extreme instances, sampling is done according to a criterion of cost. It has been the burden of the argument above that for incompletely specified models or where errors of measurement are important, observations collected in this way will frequently have greater relevance for studying gross characteristics of behavior than would result from unrestricted random sampling procedures.

1.2. Lag Effects and the Extreme Instance. Even supposing that *ceteris paribus* considerations are unimportant, difficulties of interpretation can arise if response lags are long or variable. By focusing on *shifts* in the level of the independent variable rather than attempting to study the effects of variations around a particular level, however, these problems also can be alleviated. That is, again we look for main effects rather than minor adjustments, and lags may be reasonably unimportant for these purposes. Shifts in the level of the independent variable can be expected to produce shifts in the level of the dependent variable whatever the pattern of lag adjustments. Thus the extreme instance can provide a particularly suitable basis for testing the comparative statics implications of a static model.

2. The Definitions of Adversity and Response

It will be recalled that both the managerial discretion models and the entrepreneurial models predicted that staff and output would be reduced in response to a downward shift in demand. In addition, expenditures on emoluments would be reduced in those managerial discretion models that included an emoluments term in the utility function.

Thus, with respect to staff and output, the comparative statics properties of the two classes of models were identical. It was suggested, however, that although the comparative statics properties were identical, that, *ceteris paribus*, the staff response would be larger in the utility maximizing firms than in the profit maximizing firms.[4] Although this result cannot be derived at a completely general level, it can be shown to be reasonable.

To make the situation most nearly comparable to that of the firms studied, assume that demand has been increasing steadily for a period of six or more years and assume that the best estimate of future demand is an extrapolation of the recent past. In these circumstances, the firm that is operated so as to maximize expected discounted profits will

---

[4] The output response would also be larger, but less noticeably—since it is due to the connection between optimal output and staff, rather than a direct response associated with the "utility" of output.

employ in any particular period a larger staff than it would have had demand been fixed at a single level in the past and was expected so to continue into the future. That is, the firm will attempt to anticipate its future-period needs for staff, and if demand has been increasing it will have a certain number of people in the process of training during the current period but who make a negligible contribution to current-period productivity. Thus, if $\bar{S}_t$ is the optimal level of staff in period t if demand were fixed and not expected to change, and if dX/dt is the rate of change of demand, then the actual level of staff that the firm maximizing discounted profits will employ in period t will be

$$S_t = \bar{S}_t + f_1\left(\frac{dX}{dt}\right)$$

where $$\frac{\partial f_1}{\partial(dX/dt)} > 0.$$

If the firm has a positive expense preference for staff, it will tend to employ more than the amount S_t. Instead, it will employ S_t plus an amount related to the size of its opportunity set (which is a function of the condition of the environment and the diffusion of the stockholders) and the strength of its preference for staff. The size of the opportunity set can be represented by the difference between maximum profit available (designated π') and the minimum profit demanded (designated π_0), that is, by the amount $\pi' - \pi_0$. The value of π_0 is assumed to be a function of the diffusion of the stockholders (designated D), so that π_0 can be represented by $\pi_0(D)$. Let the taste of the management for staff be represented by V and the total employment of staff by S_t^V. Then the utility maximizing firm will employ

$$S_t^V = \bar{S}_t + f_1\left(\frac{dX}{dt}\right) + f_2[\pi' - \pi_0(D), V]$$

where $\dfrac{\partial f_2}{\partial[\pi' - \pi_0(D)]} > 0$ and $\partial f_2/\partial V > 0$.

Adversity in the firms studied generally involved a cessation of the rate of increase in demand rather than an actual drop in demand. Thus, after a long period during which $dX/dt > 0$, the firm entered a period during which $dX/dt = 0$. Under these circumstances, the discounted profit maximizing firm will tend to adjust S_t toward $\bar{S}_t$. The utility maximizing firm, however, has an additional adjustment to make if, simultaneously, the firm's profitability drops. In each of the firms investigated, this pairing of a leveling off in demand together with a drop in profitability did occur, and this constituted the "adversity" with which the firms were confronted.

The size of the adjustment due to the operation of expense preference will depend on (1) the change in the shape of the profit-as-a-function-of-staff curve; (2) the change in π' relative to $\pi_0(D)$; and (3) the tastes of the management for staff, V.

It is assumed that the profit-as-a-function-of-staff curve has as minimum curvature the shape that it had prior to adversity; that is, the profit-as-a-function-of-staff curve after the onset of adversity is either a displacement without change in curvature of the curve prior to adversity, or the curve is more sharply peaked.[5] It is also assumed that the absolute change in $\pi_0(D)$ is smaller than the change in π'; that is, $\pi_0(D)$ is assumed to move within narrower bounds than π'.

Under these circumstances, the resulting profit-as-a-function-of-staff curve will be shifted vertically downwards, or downwards and to the left, as a result of adversity. The vertical displacement condition is the easier to treat graphically, and its results generalize without difficulty (Figure 1). Under these conditions, the profit maximizing level of

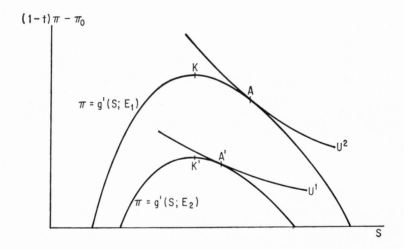

Figure 1

---

[5] Actually, the more sharply peaked condition seems the more reasonable, but it is sufficient to claim no change in curvature to support the argument. The curve would be more sharply peaked if, as seems likely, the marginal value product of staff at every level of staff beyond the profit maximizing value (S_K), falls as a result of adversity.

staff S_K is unchanged, but there will be a reduction in staff due to the expense preference effect, since the marginal rate of substitution of profit for staff $\dfrac{\partial U/\partial S}{\partial U/\partial \pi}$ falls as profit falls. That is, the curvature of the indifference curves shift so as to provide a tangency between the profit curve and the indifference curves at a lower value of staff after adversity sets in rather than previously. Thus, $S_{A'}$ is necessarily less than S_A under these conditions.

Of course the magnitude of the shift in staff depends on the drop in π' relative to $\pi_0(D)$ (which is shown by the difference from K to K') and the taste of the management for staff. If the taste for staff is relatively large, then at high levels of profit the indifference curves will be comparatively steep and, *ceteris paribus*, the tangency A will occur rather far to the right of K. The taste effects are much less detectable at low levels of profit, however, since the indifference curves are assumed to be asymptotic to the horizontal axis. Hence, the effect of taste shows up mainly at the high profitability levels where the indifference curves will be more (less) steeply sloped, and the optimal choice of staff more (less) removed from the profit maximizing value S_K, depending on the strength of the taste for staff. The same type of argument carries over to the analysis of the situation where adversity results not merely in a downward shift in the profit as a function of staff curve, but a shift of this curve to the left as well, although the analysis of curvatures becomes somewhat more involved.[6] In general, however, the staff adjustment of the utility maximizing firm will again exceed that of the profit maximizing firm and for the same reasons.

A similar, although somewhat stronger, argument can be applied to expenditures on emoluments. As defined, these are economic rents that are removed by the management from the firm's profits. In a profit maximizing organization operated entirely in the stockholders' interests, these will be zero; that is, salary, expense accounts, executive services, and so forth will reach the competitive level but will not exceed it. In a utility maximizing organization, these expenditures will exceed the competitive levels in proportion to the difference between π'

---

[6] The analysis would be complicated if substantial changes in output occurred as a result of adversity. In the firms reported here, this did not occur. If such changes did occur, an assumption about the shape of the production cost curve would be required. It would facilitate the argument if average production costs were constant or increased as output was reduced.

and $\pi_0(D)$ and the taste of the management for emoluments (designated W). That is,

$$M = g[\pi' - \pi_0(D), W]$$

where $\dfrac{\partial g}{\partial[\pi' - \pi_0(D)]} > 0$ and $\partial g/\partial W > 0$.

In the firm where no emoluments are extracted (that is, where $M = 0$), the stabilization of demand accompanied by a fall in π' relative to $\pi_0(D)$ will tend to leave salary, expense accounts, executive services, and so forth unchanged. These will be continued at the level dictated by competitive and profit considerations. Assuming that the marginal contributions for which these expenditures are payments are essentially unchanged, the expenditures will tend to be fixed. In a firm with a positive preference for emoluments, however, a reduction in emoluments will occur in these circumstances. For reasons entirely similar to those discussed above, this reduction is due to the decrease in the marginal rate of substitution of profit for emoluments $\left(\dfrac{\partial U/\partial\pi}{\partial U/\partial M}\right)$ as profit falls. And again this manifests itself in a flattening of the indifference curves at lower levels of profit. Hence tangency occurs at a lower level of emoluments as a result of the decline in profitability.[7]

To summarize, the profit maximizing firm will reduce staff when the rate of increase in demand declines and expectations (which are assumed to be positively related to dX/dt) develop that this condition will persist. The utility maximizing firm with a positive preference for staff will make this same adjustment plus an additional reduction, the magnitude of which will depend on the character of its indifference surface and the severity of the associated profit decline. The profit maximizing firm in which the management has been extracting no emoluments will make no adjustment in emoluments as a result of adversity. In a utility maximizing organization with a positive preference for emoluments, however, emoluments will be reduced in response to adversity, and again the magnitude of the adjustment will depend on the shape of the indifference surface and the severity of the associated profit decline.

---

[7] This can be shown geometrically using Figure 5 in Chapter 4. Adversity merely entails shifting the line connecting maximal combinations of profit and emoluments vertically downward. It follows directly from the marginal rate of substitution effects described above that emoluments will be reduced.

3. Chemical Products Incorporated

Size: Chemical Products Inc. is a specialty chemical company. Annual sales of the parent company have been about 200 million dollars and employment, prior to the recent cutbacks, has numbered about 10,000.

Control: The company was largely the creation of one man, and the family still controls about 40 per cent of the common stock outstanding. Until recently, heirs of the founder occupied over half of the positions on the board of directors and held almost all of the top executive posts in the organization.

Adversity: The sector of the industry serviced by the company had, in the words of its current president, enjoyed a seller's market "for over 80 per cent of the last century .... We became accustomed to being able to sell all we could produce." With the exception of a 7 per cent decline in sales in 1948 and a 3 per cent decline in 1952, the company enjoyed steadily increasing sales between 1947 and 1956. During this interval, sales increased by 150 per cent and operating profit as a percentage of sales fluctuated between 15 and 23 per cent, with a mean of 19 per cent.

Sales stabilized in 1957 and operating profit as a percentage of sales dropped from 18 to 14 per cent. Sales were unchanged in 1958, but the profit rate on sales fell to just over 9 per cent. Although sales increased by 16 per cent in 1959, the profit rate on sales was slightly under 10 per cent.

By 1960 it was evident that the condition of excess capacity that had developed in the industry would be a continuing one; prices were unlikely to be increased soon. If profits were to be improved, the improvement would have to come from another source. Thus, in June 1960, a few months after a new president had been installed in office, a broad assault on the entire cost structure was mounted.

3.1. Phase One: Cost Reduction.   A substantial reorganization among the top management personnel accompanied the installation of the new president. This meant more than regrouping existing functions under existing executives. It also involved the placement of new officers in almost all of the top executive positions. The company, therefore, undertook the cost reduction program with neither the chief executive's post nor those of his immediate subordinates occupied by holdovers. This action naturally severed a certain connection with and commitment to past actions and gave the company greater flexibility in developing its response to adversity. In particular, it provided incentive to begin its cost reduction efforts "at the top," which is by no means the typical sequence.

The cost reduction program had as its objective the "elimination of unprofitable and unproductive projects." Basically, this entailed a removal of personnel, a reduction in or redirection of spending on certain discretionary activities, and the elimination of a number of expenditures on emoluments.

Within nine months the number of employees had been cut by 20 per cent. This produced annual savings, before taxes, estimated at more than 10 million dollars. Further reductions have since been possible so that two years after the inception of the program, *with production unchanged*, the company reported:

1. *Return on investment: increased by 125* per cent.[8]
2. *Breakeven* point: *reduced* from 95 to 74 per cent.
3. Total *employment: decreased* by 25 per cent; salaried employees reduced by 32 per cent, hourly by 20 per cent.
4. *Payrolls: reduced* by 16 per cent or 12 million dollars.
5. *Overhead: reduced* from 14 million dollars to 12 million dollars and scheduled to go to 8 million dollars.
6. *Headquarters employment: reduced* from 782 to 462 (with plans to decrease it to 362).

Research and development was subjected to particularly severe scrutiny in the new emphasis on being "selective in our activities and profit oriented in our work." On evaluating the research and development program it was found that the company had spent 15 million dollars for R and D in the preceding ten years but had produced hardly anything in the way of profitable results. Of the 700 active projects, only four were found worthy of continuation. However, this cutback on internally sponsored research and development did not mean that the company abandoned its R and D effort. Rather, it reduced its staff of 165 personnel to 52 and redirected much of its work to commercial R and D companies.

---

[8] The financial reports of the subsidiaries were consolidated with those of the parent company in 1960, and it is not possible, from the firm's annual reports, to break out the performance of the parent company on an operating income as a percentage-of-sales basis as was done above. However, the officers in the firm estimate that the return on investment has increased from 4 to 9 per cent (these figures apply to parent company performance only). The return is calculated on the accounting valuation of the firm's assets.

Although total expenditure for research and development has scarcely changed, the emphasis has clearly shifted.

Personnel and public relations was another activity for which particularly severe reductions were made. The staff was reduced from 57 to 7 but without, in the opinion of its new department head, impairing its ability to provide any of its essential services. Some activities, such as photography services, were discontinued, but this had the effect of requiring division managers to consider the cost of such services before requesting them. As a result, the demand for activities previously provided at no (apparent) cost has substantially declined.

Re-examination of product lines led to the disposal of certain subsidiaries, and a review of distribution practices produced the decision to discontinue national advertising. Distribution, however, played a major role in the reconstruction phase described below.

The biggest reductions in overhead resulted from the elimination of staffs and the associated savings in salaries. As pointed out earlier, headquarters employment has been reduced from 782 to 462 (with plans to decrease it to 362). However, the elimination of emoluments has also importantly contributed to the overhead reduction. Among the emoluments previously provided but now removed or reduced are

1. The company fleet of airplanes has been disposed of.
2. The company car and chauffeur service has been discontinued.
3. The executive dining service has been discontinued.
4. Travel and entertainment expenses have been reduced.
5. The New York and Washington, D.C., suites and offices have been eliminated.
6. Private secretaries among middle-rank executives have been replaced by group secretaries in a ratio of about 3 to 1.

3.2. Phase Two: Reconstruction. The cost reduction program has recently given way to a longer range program designed to assure that the benefits realized will not be dissipated. Cost control via better methods and standards is being emphasized. In addition, improvements in the quality of the staffs is taking place. Greater attention is given to market research and profit planning, and an operations research staff has been created. Most important of all, however, has been the company's emphasis on distribution. Several large distributing organizations were acquired, giving the company more direct access to the market with its own products and permitting it to serve as a distribution agent for other manufacturers. Together with the improved efficiency of the organization, it is believed that this added flexibility will prevent a recurrence of the situation that developed in the late 1950's.

3.3. Evaluation. As was indicated earlier in Section 2, the multi-period profit maximizing organization that has been training people for staff positions in anticipation of a continuing increase in demand will have occasion to remove some of these personnel if the increase in demand fails to materialize. This description appears to hold in the case of Chemical Products Inc. Hence, a reduction in staff based on the decline in the rate of change of demand (dX/dt) would be predicted.

Although this accounts for the direction of change that occurred in the company, the magnitudes are sufficiently large to raise a question over whether they too can be explained on this basis. How is a reduction of 41 per cent in headquarters employment made consistent with a reduction in the rate of increase of sales from about 10 per cent a year to 0 per cent? Possibly such a reconciliation can be performed without invoking the notion of expense preference.[9] But clearly the explanation is much less difficult to provide if it is assumed that the firm displayed a positive preference for staff in the period preceding the profit decline.

If positive expense preference toward staff is assumed, then the firm will increase the employment of staff over the profit maximizing level in relation to the difference between the maximum profit available (π') and the minimum profit demanded $[\pi_0(D)]$, and in accordance with its taste for staff (V). Clearly the condition of excess capacity in the industry and the resulting weakening in prices led to a decline in π'. It also seems reasonable to assume that $\pi_0(D)$ declined by a smaller amount. Thus the difference $\pi' - \pi_0(D)$ would fall, and this would produce a reduction in the amount of staff that could be supported by the expense preference term.

---

[9] Assuming the firm had been operated so as to maximize the discounted stream of future profits, a sizeable reduction could occur if the firm encountered its minimum profit constraint as a result of adversity (see the discussion of this in Section 1.2 of Chapter 5). Although the management of Chemical Products Inc. insists that they are not sacrificing future profits for the sake of current, this is difficult to document. Observing the places in the organization where the cuts were particularly sharp is probably of some relevance. Thus, the R and D staff was reduced by 68 per cent, most of the current projects suspended, and much of its research was contracted out. In personnel and public relations, the staff was reduced by 88 per cent. Since R and D expenditures were maintained, it is somewhat difficult to argue that future benefits have been entirely neglected. In personnel and public relations, both the size of the staff and its appropriation were reduced. Although this may be partly at the expense of future period profits, it is awkward to explain the whole of this enormous reduction in this way.

This adjustment was made all the more vigorous by the change in "tastes" that accompanied the cost reduction program. As pointed out, a new president and a number of new officers were installed just prior to the initiation of the cost reduction program. In 1959 five of the seven top executives were heirs of the founder. In 1961 only one of these remained. In particular, the vice presidents of research and development and personnel and public relations were replaced. Similarly, five of the nine positions on the board of directors were occupied by heirs in 1959, and this was reduced to four positions on an expanded 12-member board in 1961. A decisive shift in the tastes of the management away from staff and towards profit could be expected of such an over-all change. Thus, a sizeable fraction of the sharp reduction in staff that was made was possibly due to the combined effects of the fall in profitability and the shift in tastes.

The reduction in expenditures on emoluments is even more difficult to accommodate under the profit maximization hypothesis. An explanation to the effect that temporary reductions in perquisites are acceptable as long as they *average* out to the competitive level might be invoked, but it is clearly *ad hoc*. However, a parallel explanation to the expense preference effects described above can accommodate these as entirely *rational* adjustments to a change in tastes and in the size of the opportunity set.

Considering the concentration of ownership and control unusual among firms of this size, the apparent profusion of staff and emoluments that occurred may seem unusual. Clearly profits have immediate relevance to the management in such circumstances. The evidence suggests, however, that pecuniary gain is not the only objective of the management, even where the linkage between profits and self-interest is so direct. Indeed, among already wealthy heirs, nonpecuniary objectives (such as status, power, prestige, and professional exellence) may be of considerable importance, and to neglect them may be the source of much confusion.

That extensive reductions in hourly workers were also achieved was less expected. It contradicts the proposition that production decisions are made according to conventional profit maximization principles and suggests that possibly "labor slack" should be allowed for in the model. However, the experience of Chemical Products Inc. may be somewhat atypical since the workers were not represented by an independent union and the company had a reputation for paternalism. The latter of these facts may have led to easy employment conditions (and thus a situation of excess hourly employees), whereas the former may explain the lack of difficulty the company encountered in redefining and combining jobs in the reorganization.

4. Midwest Processing Corporation

Size: Midwest Processing Corporation is a major producer of industrial and consumer products. Annual sales run to several hundred million dollars and its work force numbers over 40 thousand.

Control: Heirs of the founders control over 40 per cent of the common stock outstanding. Although they dominate the board of directors, they have not placed one of their kind in the top executive's post for over 10 years.

Adversity: The company has a long and impressive record of growth and earnings. In earlier periods this was partly due to the favorable market position that the company enjoyed. More recently, the vigorous growth of demand has helped sustain earnings. Perhaps as important as each of these, however, has been the generally excellent management of the company.[10] Although this may not have prevented the company from developing slack during its periods of high earnings, it may help explain why the slack did not become more extensive than it did as well as why the organization reacted as soon as it did to the onset of adversity.

With the single exception of 1949, sales increased continuously between 1948 and 1956, with 1956 sales being almost exactly double the 1948 level. Operating profit as a percentage of sales during the period ranged between 11 and 22 per cent, the mean being 18 per cent.

A general anticipation that demand in the late 1950's would continue to grow at the earlier rate led to a serious condition of excess capacity in 1957. By mid-1957, according to one of the firm's officers, it was "obvious that competitive and general business conditions [had] created a serious need to reduce operating and administrative costs." Operating profit as a percentage of sales fell from the 21 per cent level realized in 1956 to 18 per cent in 1957. This dropped to 12 per cent in 1958, remained at that level in 1959, dropped again in 1960 to 6 per cent, and increased to 8 per cent in 1961. Sales during this five-year interval were essentially unchanged from the 1956 level (with the exception of 1958 when sales were off by 13 per cent).

---

[10] Rankings by the American Institute of Management are hardly widely enough accepted to be considered authoritative. It may nonetheless be of some significance that the company's management has been rated "excellent" by this group.

Since cost control had been left largely up to the individual administrative and operating units (the company had no comprehensive budget program in 1957), an *ad hoc* committee was created for the explicit purpose of reviewing costs and achieving appropriate reductions. This turned out to be the first step in what later developed into a three-phase program.

4.1. Phase One: Cost Reduction. The company had never previously encountered a situation where profits were seriously threatened and had no previous experience with cost reduction programs. It did, however, have the benefit of perceptiveness in the controller's office. Rather than attempt an across-the-board reduction, they chose instead to tailor their efforts. Of particular significance are the criteria for selection that were employed. Thus the decision of where to cut was guided by the management's observation that

> In any large organization, certain plants or departments will have found ways to habitually operate more efficiently than others. This may be due to *competitive pressure* which has historically been felt in some products to a greater extent than others. It may also be due to differences in *individual management philosophy* .... It follows ... that any approach toward an arbitrary management dictate for an across-the-board slash in all cost areas will inevitably damage necessary functions in some areas, and leave remaining inefficiencies in others. (Italics added.)

The *ad hoc* committee achieved a 20 per cent reduction in employment within the operating divisions over a period of about eight months. This entailed the release of about 10,000 employees. Only token reductions in headquarters employment were attempted at this time.

Details of this operation have never been released by the company. However, the experience of two of their divisions, said to be reasonably representative of the entire organization, provide some insights on this matter.

DIVISION A

Employed in:	Percentage of Total Released
Support departments	40
Operating departments	60
Total	100

Within the Support Departments

Employed as:	Percentage of Total Support Released
Supervisory	5
Professional	4
Technical	45
Clerical	29
Custodial	17
Total	100

Within the Operating Departments

Employed as:	Percentage of Total Operating Released
Supervisory	11
Professional	1
Technical	2
Clerical	7
Custodial	1
Direct labor	78*
Total	100

* The chairman of the *ad hoc* committee claims that most of these resulted directly from the drop in 1958 production and were not due to the efforts of the committee.

DIVISION B

The data were incomplete for the Division B operating departments. It appears, however, that the reductions were split about evenly between support and operating. The following changes occurred within the support departments:

Employed as:	Percentage of Total Support Released
Supervisory	6
Professional	12
Technical	26
Clerical	44
Custodial	12
Total	100

The support departments provide such services as personnel, purchasing, plant engineering, maintenance, accounting, etc. Salaried personnel in the operating divisions typically represent 25 per cent of the work force. Of the categories above, they occupy the positions designated as supervisory, professional, and clerical, as well as about two-thirds of the technical. With the exception of supervisory, these are, approximately, the operating division "staff." Supervisory employees are department heads or foremen; professional include engineering, legal, and some specialized managerial; clerical are secretarial and accounting; technical are purchasing, inspection, laboratory, maintenance, planning, and drafting.

The data from Divisions A and B indicate that reductions among support personnel were particularly extensive. Discussions with the chief budgeting officer revealed that this was the general pattern throughout the operating divisions. Thus, he observed that

1. The employment of staff in the operating divisions has an inherent tendency to expand unless subjected to careful review.
2. Intensive review had not been provided prior to the cost reduction program.
3. It was largely salaried employees who were affected by the *ad hoc* committee review.
4. Since the work of hourly employees is typically subjected to continuing analysis in an effort to improve standards and techniques, only modest cutbacks beyond those normally made were obtained within the hourly production group.
5. Labor agreements prohibiting the consolidation of jobs tend to limit cutbacks among hourly employees, whereas this constraint is not encountered within the salaried ranks.

4.2. Phase Two: Control Budgets in the Operating Divisions.
As was remarked earlier, the company had no comprehensive budgeting system but relied on the individual divisions to plan their own activities and coordinate these as the need arose according to the nature of the problem. It was decided, however, that the "crash program" that had been undertaken "would not be permanently effective unless it was followed up by a permanent, self-policing system of cost control." Approximately two years after the cost reduction program had been initiated, a control budget system was developed. It was installed in the plants over a period of 15 months. By December 1960, control budgets were in use in all of the operating divisions.

The manufacturing budget system is not an advanced one and is still being articulated. Evaluations of it are very difficult to come by. However, it is felt that "in the short period during which [it] has been in effect, there has been a noticeable trend of decreasing unfavorable budget variations and . . . tightening of budgets and standards."

4.3. Phase Three: Control Budgets for Administrative and Selling Expense. Administrative and selling expense at the headquarters unit was virtually untouched by the cost reduction program, and the plant control budget likewise left headquarters spending intact. However, pressure for profit improvement continued. Operating profits in 1960 were only about one-third of those previously earned on comparable volume.

It thus became apparent that additional reductions would be required. Attention was therefore turned to headquarters expenses. That these should be left until last was, with the benefit of hindsight, recognized as a poor strategy. That is, over the entire period during which the crash program and control budgets were being introduced into the operating divisions, headquarters had at best made but token reductions in forces. In fact, aggregate headquarters employment in December 1960 was 10 per cent *over* the level of December 1958. This was a source of some resentment among the operating divisions and possibly prevented the cost reductions within the divisions from being as extensive as they might otherwise have been.

In January 1961 a control budget for headquarters expenditures was introduced. Its effect was immediate. The principal reductions in general administrative and selling expense occurred in salaries, traveling expense, advertising, and legal and professional fees, in that order. Not only did the 1961 reductions arrest the steady trend of rising headquarters expenditures, but an actual reduction of 8 per cent from the level of 1960 expenditures was realized. "Comparing the original forecast of 1961 expenditures made by each department head in December with the ... approved budgets, ... it would appear that *this program alone will save the company over 5 million dollars in 1961.*" (Italics added.)

Using December 1958 as a base, general administrative and selling expense employment has undergone the following changes:

Number of Personnel as
Percentage of December 1958

	December 1958	December 1959	December 1960	October 1961
Administrative	100	103	108	100
Research and development	100	105	110	97
Selling	100	103	111	98
Total G. A. and S. E. employment	100	103	110	99

By way of providing perspective, it may be useful to note:

1. As of October 1961, administrative represented 34 per cent, research 20 per cent, and selling 46 per cent of total personnel accounted for as general administrative and selling expense.
2. Sales in 1961 were 99 per cent of those in 1960 and 113 per cent of those in 1958.
3. Based on the recent trend of headquarters employment, the (linear) projected 1961 rate would be 113 per cent of 1958. This makes the actual rate of 99 per cent all the more impressive.

By no means were all of the 5 million dollar savings due to reductions in force. Expenditures for many items were reduced and planned additions curtailed or postponed. Traveling expense is an example of the former; it was reduced from 1960 levels by 18 per cent at the sales offices and 40 per cent at the home office. Moreover, the company feels that this reduction has not in the least impaired its sales effectiveness. (Some reports indicate that it has led to both better customer relations and a better image for the organization.) Another example of an expense reduction is advertising. It was reduced by 10 per cent from its 1960 level.

An example of a postponement in expenditures brought about by the administrative expense control budget is provided in a speech by the chief budgeting officer:

[The company] executives thought our administrative budget was too high last year, and one of the temporarily expendable items was found to be a planned electronic computer installation which was one of my favorite projects. Finding myself in the untenable position of being author of the budget system and preaching the principles which I am outlining tonight, while I was also administrator of the electronic computer program, there was obviously nothing to do but duck. The serious lesson to be learned here is that we *did* delay the computer project for one year, we did thereby save over 300,000 thousand dollars in that year, and we still found a way of continuing our data processing mechanization program by utilizing spare time on a computer located at one of our plants. It wasn't easy; *if we had not been faced with the necessity*, we would have brushed it off as impractical. But necessity is the mother of invention, and an aggresive budget program causes everyone to think of alternative, better and cheaper ways to accomplish their purpose.

I could spend the rest of this evening with specific cases where our people found ways to accomplish just as much for less money. (Italics added.)

4.4. Evaluation. Again a high concentration of ownership prevailed. Unlike Chemical Products Inc., the major stockholders in Midwest Processing Corporation did not place their own numbers in top management positions in the firm but rather exercised their control from the board of directors. Judging from the comparative adjustments within these two firms, this seems to favor closer conformance to profit considerations than does active management participation by the heirs.

Although this generalization is not warranted by the analysis of these two firms alone, it does have some a priori appeal. When the owners are active as managers, they are simultaneously subject to two not altogether consistent interests. As owners they favor attention to profit goals; as managers they are interested in advancing personal goals, which may include nonpecuniary elements. A compromise that reflects tastes and environmental conditions will result. Thus, if competition in the product market is not severe, and if tastes favor expansion, the manager-stockholder may feel entirely free to pursue these goals. When the ownership confines itself to representation on the board of directors, however, it is less apt to treat the firm as a source of important nonpecuniary satisfactions. The management may still pursue expansionary objectives, but the attention to profit is likely to be enhanced.

Other aspects of the field study that are of interest for obtaining insights "into the essentials of the situation" are

1. The criteria that were used in choosing the areas in which cost reductions could be made reveal that the management explicitly discriminated both on the basis of competition in the product market and management philosophy (tastes) in deciding which divisions should have costs reduced. These are precisely the factors that are responsible for discretionary behavior in the managerial model.
2. Although there is not sufficient detail to evaluate the cuts in the operating division staff on the basis of the model developed in Section 2, the adjustments appear to be sizeable and, taken together with the criteria mentioned above, appear to be consistent with those that would be expected in a utility maximizing organization that displayed a positive preference for staff and found itself confronted by adversity.

3. The sequence with which the cost reduction program proceeded is of interest. First, cost reductions in the operating divisions were demanded by the top management. Consolidation and extension of these cost reductions through the introduction of control budgets in the operating divisions followed. Only when these efforts failed to produce the desired improvement in profit did top management examine its own expenditure levels. That is, the headquarters group continued, as long as it could, those expenditures most closely related to its own satisfactions. This behavior is consistent with the March and Simon observation that "opportunistic changes in the inducements-contributions balance of an organization will tend to leave untouched those inducements and contributions that are objects of identification of the individuals initiating change" [81, p. 109]. Although such behavior is not comprehended by the static managerial discretion model, it suggests the need to introduce lag adjustments into a dynamic model and defer cuts in headquarters staff and emoluments until other reductions fail to produce the cost savings required. As the analysis of Chemical Products Inc. indicates, this is probably not an essential elaboration when the cost reduction efforts are accompanied by a major change in top executive personnel.

4. The relation of cost consciousness to "necessity," as revealed in the speech of the chief budgeting officer, is of interest. In the absence of binding constraints, "favorite projects" apparently obtain approval with ease. When profit objectives are incompletely realized, however, nonexpansionary alternatives are given greater consideration. Unless profit is inversely correlated with time available to evaluate alternatives, such behavior is not easily accommodated by the profit maximizing hypothesis but is generally to be expected in the utility maximizing organization.

5. General Manufacturing Company

Size: General Manufacturing Company is a major producer of durable goods. Its annual sales exceed three-quarters of a billion dollars, and its work force numbers over 75,000.

Control: In 1957 the General Manufacturing Company had over 100,000 stockholders with ownership distributed as follows: Of the total shares outstanding, 88 per cent were held by stockholders owning from 1 to 100 shares; 10 per cent were held by stockholders owning from 101 to 500 shares; 1 per cent were held by stockholders owning 501 to 1000 shares; 1 per cent were held by stockholders owning over 1001 shares. The largest single holding of any officer of the company amounted to less than one-twentieth of 1 per cent. Only one-fourth of the seats on the board of directors are currently occupied by officers in the company.

Adversity: With the exception of 1949, when sales dropped by 3 per cent, sales increased continuously over the interval 1947 to 1954—1954 sales being just over twice those realized in 1947. Operating profit as a percentage of sales ranged from 10 to 15 per cent during the interval, the mean being 12 per cent. In 1955 sales dropped by 12 per cent and the operating profit rate fell to 6 per cent. Sales improved in 1956, reached an all-time high in 1957, dropped by 5 per cent in 1958, and remained at this level through 1961. During this interval, operating profit as a percentage of sales varied between 0 and 7 per cent, the mean being 5 per cent.

Although the company as a whole has been under sustained pressure to improve its profit position, the pressure has not been equally severe across all of the company's operating divisions. Some operating divisions have continued to enjoy very sizeable profits; others have succeeded only in just getting by; still others have consistently produced losses. Since there were substantial dissimilarities between the products manufactured, the markets served, and the earnings produced by the company's divisions, there was a distinct advantage in studying its "profit centers" separately rather than as an aggregate. The company was very cooperative in providing the type of information necessary for this purpose.

In order to achieve better coordination and control over its operations, General Manufacturing Company has introduced the most comprehensive budgeting and review system of any of the firms examined. Indeed, it is a leader among U. S. firms in the development of profit planning and cost control techniques. This desire to gain control at the top while operating an otherwise decentralized organization manifests itself in several ways. The most important consequence is that the managers of the operating divisions sit down with top management once each year to *bargain* over their profit goals and expenditure levels for the coming year. Past performance plays a critical role in determining the extent to which division managers successfully negotiate their objectives. A second effect of this attempt to gain control are the dysfunctional consequences (such as the deliberate misclassification of expense) that it occasionally produces.

5.1. *A Statement of the Company Approach.* Internal documents in the company that describe the objectives and procedures of the budgeting program provide a useful record of how top management, and in particular the budgeting authority, views the problem of cost control and profit improvement. Special attention should be given to the *language* used to explain their objectives.

The following observations and instructions were prepared by the budgeting officer second-in-command for a company document describing objectives:

1. Earnings, the ultimate goals of long range planning, easily become the victim of unbridled growth in expenditures for various corporate functions aside from direct production. [In commenting on this statement, the writer indicated that it was staff activities that he had in mind and that the inherent tendency for managers to increase staff presents a continuous threat to the achievement of profit goals.]

2. Divisions are urged to follow a sequence of thought and planning which will result in objectives which will lift performance and effort to new levels. Basically, this sequence is to *establish an objective profit performance first, and then to work backwards to specific cost and expense objectives* which will result in the profit desired, but at the same time encompass a maximum effort toward building for the future.

3. With the objective rate of return on investment and a projection of the required investment in gross assets, it is now possible to determine the dollar level of profit which will be required to attain the objective rate of return. Having determined this, the dollars of profit desired can be subtracted from the expected revenue from sales to obtain the allowable level of total cost. The subtraction of the minimum obtainable level of necessary operating costs ... then results in determination of *funds available* for expenditures on improvement programs and other types of policy costs.

   Obviously such a procedure may result either in no funds being available for policy costs under existing circumstances or funds in an amount which is clearly too low for adequate improvement programs to safeguard the future of the product. If this happens, two alternatives present themselves.

   (1) *Reduce* planned operating costs sufficiently to finance the needed policy costs. (2) If this is not practical then it

becomes necessary to revise the plan so that the objective rate of return will be accomplished over a longer period of time than that covered by the existing plan. It results in the establishment of interim objectives which are steps toward the ultimate objective, but which, for the period in question, may be somewhat less than the final goal.

As in the final step, it is management's job to plan the use of funds which are available for basic improvement activities so that the maximum contribution to future profits is obtained.

4. It is vitally important that the projection of markets and/or division participation in those markets be *completely realistic* since it is to serve as the basis for the planning of cost and expense levels. It is the [current] policy of our company, in fact to lean on the conservative side in projecting future sales for profit planning purposes in order that expense levels may be kept on a minimum basis.

Indeed, the company has since resorted to two sales forecasts: one for planning sales and a lower one for planning expenses. This was felt necessary to impose control over the level of expenses. Thus, in a guide to the divisions designed to help them prepare their budgets appears the statement:

It is desirable to select a conservative volume level, in order to induce tight planning of expense levels. Typically, the volume selected for financial planning purposes will be below the market projection, and below the objectives set for sales department performance. (Italics, wherever used in the quotations above, have been added.)

The statements lead to a number of insights into the company's problems and its methods of dealing with them. Thus the following comments appear warranted:

1. Quotation 1 provides a clear statement of the need to hold expenditures on staff in check. It also reveals that direct costs, typically, are not as likely to get out of line—being subject, as they are, to continuing scrutiny much of the time.

2. Quotation 2 is an indication of how the headquarters unit is able to obtain desired performance among the divisions by negotiating an "objective profit performance." This then becomes the basis for deter-

mining cost and expense levels. Hopefully these will produce the objective performance intended.

3. Quotation 3 develops in more detail the way that profit goals and cost and expense categories interact. Subtracting profit goals from expected sales (where these are apparently derived from projections of trend) yields the aggregate level of cost and expense allowable. Subtracting from this the "minimum obtainable" level of operating costs then determines the amount of discretionary spending on expense items that can be supported.

These residual funds may be less than required (a possibility recognized in the statement), or they may be greater than the division, relative to other profit centers in the company, can properly justify (a possibility that goes unmentioned). In the former case, an effort is made to reduce (minimum?) cost even further and, this failing, a revision in objectives is made.[11]

Where excess residual funds are generated, the division has in the past been permitted to spend them as it chose. However, there is no necessary relation between a division's need for policy-type expenditures and the volume of funds it generates for this purpose. Indeed, the divisions which, from the standpoint of the company, could most profitably use these discretionary funds may be precisely the divisions that fail to provide them out of their own operations. To remedy this obvious defect, the company is attempting this year to pool the available policy funds and allocate them according to what are felt to be the best interests of the company taken as a whole. There is, however, a widespread feeling that this plan will eventually be scrapped. In the words of one of the division coordinators, "It will provide a division that wanted to spend its discretionary funds internally but was required to release them with an excuse whenever its subsequent performance deteriorates. That is, the division will say that it cannot be held accountable for this change in fortune; had they been permitted to spend the funds that were properly theirs, this unfortunate turn of events could have been avoided." Unwarranted though the argument be, it may be difficult to refute. Hence the dilemma of distributing discretionary funds is expected to persist.

4. The fourth quotation indicates how deliberate biases are introduced into the planning process in the full knowledge of the planners. Cost and expense budgets are based on conservative projections of sales while the objectives set for the sales department are more optimistic.

---

[11] The conformity of this description to the Cyert and March decision process is striking [38, pp. 84–86].

Asked whether this intended bias would be compensated for in division requests for expenditures, the answer was "not entirely"—but, apparently, previous cost histories and comparison among divisions and with competitors can be used to check any such tendency.

5.2. The Approach. As was remarked earlier, General Manufacturing Company was very cooperative in making accounting records of its divisions available for inspection. Since the firm is a decentralized one and the product line is highly diversified, this was a distinct advantage. Decentralization meant that division policy was largely determined at the division level, subject only to constraints from headquarters. Extensive product diversity meant that the separate divisions might be experiencing distinctly different market conditions; hence, to examine only aggregates could be misleading. There was, however, an associated disadvantage: descriptive detail with which to interpret the divisional records was not easily available. As a result, a crude model for evaluating divisional performance was devised, and this, together with the record of the predictions obtained from it, was submitted to the chief budgeting officials in the organization for comment. This precaution was felt necessary in order to make sure that the model properly reflected gross characteristics of performance and to correct any predictions which, due to circumstances unknown to me, were unwarranted.

The following verbal model was submitted to the chief budgeting officers in the General Manufacturing Company. Their comments are shown in brackets.

1. Direct costs are typically subject to continuous scrutiny and hence are kept at near minimum levels. [COMMENT: This is not necessarily the case in markets where price is subject to the division's control, i.e., where competition is weak.]
2. Staffs have a tendency (both legitimate and natural) to extend the scope of their activities and will proceed to do so unless confronted with constraints.
3. Binding constraints are difficult to impose on divisions where overall performance has been favorable.
4. Thus indirect costs (quite apart from inflationary and substitution trends) tend to grow under favorable conditions.
5. As a result, when the division encounters adversity and profit goals are not being met, reductions in the levels of indirect costs are usually needed in order to restore profitable performance. [COMMENT: direct costs get closer attention too.]
6. The amount and timing of the adjustment will be a function of

the division management and the division's history: other things being equal, new division managers will be more prompt to reduce indirect costs than managers who have been with the division longer; also, divisions with a long history of successful performance will be more apt to treat their indirect cost structures as institutionalized and thus will be less ready to reduce them.

In general, the model was considered an appropriate summary of the *gross* characteristics of cost and division manager behavior.

5.3. The Data. Owing to the dependency of the analysis on accounting data (which was only occasionally supplemented by special studies that had been requested by headquarters), it was felt unwise to claim as "predictions" those divisions with records that conformed to the model but for which alternative explanations could be easily provided. For example, if a division had a record of growing sales volume and respectable earnings, substantial growth in staff expense would be predicted by the managerial discretion model. But staff would also be expected to grow using the entrepreneurial model. Lacking descriptive detail, I did not feel confident in saying when such expansion exceeded amounts consistent with the latter hypothesis or fell short of that expected by the former. Similarly, when profits and sales fell simultaneously, a reduction in staff would be predicted by both models and the same difficulty was encountered. Cases of both types were treated as "simple conformance" and are not included in the data reported below.

"Extreme conformance" was taken to be any division that either (1) had high or rising profits, declining sales, and increasing staff expense or (2) had low or falling profits, increasing sales, and declining staff expense. Thus, consider the model for determining staff expenditures suggested in Section 2; namely,

$$S_t^v = \bar{S}_t + f_1\left(\frac{dX}{dt}\right) + f_2[\pi' - \pi_0(D),\ V]$$

If π' is rising relative to $\pi_0(D)$ while sales are falling, then the only component in the expression above that would support an increase in S_t^v is the last term; the first two would require that staff be reduced. Similarly, if π' is falling relative to $\pi_0(D)$ while sales are rising, then the only component that would require a decrease in S_t^v is the last term; the first two would lead to an increase in staff. Extreme conformance was taken to be any time where the discretionary allocation term not just moderated the adjustment due to changes in the volume of activity, but actually reversed the direction of adjustment.

"Contradictions" were divisions that fell into either of the two categories above but did not behave as predicted.

Operating results over the interval 1957 to 1961 were examined. Although it would have been desirable to consider a longer period, such data were neither readily nor reasonably uniformly available. The shortness of the time period is a disadvantage since many divisions did not experience significant changes in their activity or performance levels in this interval.

Of the divisions examined, five appear to conform to the model, two provide apparent contradictions, three can be explained only as exceptional performers, and the remainder did not experience sufficient change to warrant a "prediction." Earnings of less than 10 per cent on total gross assets were considered poor, earnings from 10 to 20 per cent were fair, from 20 to 30 per cent were good, and above 30 per cent were exceptional.[12]

Since the emphasis will be on indirect costs and reference will be made to changes in the composition of these expenditures, the following breakdown provides a useful perspective:

| | Expense Category | | |
Indirect Cost Type	Largely Policy	Partly Policy	Operating
1. Manufacturing			
Organ, and other operating expense			X
Plant facilities expense	X		
Manufacturing development	X		
2. Product development			
Customer order engineering			X
Product development engineering	X		
Shop tooling	X		
3. Marketing			
Division advertising and sales promotion	X		
Division and region sales		X	
Division order serv., whse., and ship.			X
4. Administrative and general		X	

---

[12] It should be noted that the division's allocation of headquarters overhead is deducted before calculation of percentage return on total gross assets. This allocation is not shown in the data presented. It is occasionally responsible for minor changes in the amount of earnings a division produces. The returns are on a before-tax basis. Also to be noted is the profit goal to which the company aspires. A 30 per cent return on total gross assets is the official long-run objective. This is widely regarded, however, as unattainable for the company as a whole.

5.3.1. Extreme Conformance

DIVISION A		As Percentage of 1957				
	1957 base	1957	1958	1959	1960	1961
Gross sales billed	100	100	106	118	141	147
Direct costs	82*	100	93	93	114	114
Indirect costs	37*	100	100	84	90	87
Percent return on total gross assets**		−29	−26	3.8	7.9	6.2
Percent market share**		6.6	7.7	7.0	7.4	7.3

    * As percentage of GSB.
  ** Actual.

Gross sales billed rose steadily from 1957 to 1961; also, direct costs moved up. Indirect costs, however, were reduced. This leads to the prediction that earnings in Division A were bad to poor. Upon inspection of the record for return on total gross assets this prediction turns out to be entirely correct. Earnings had been negative during the first two years in the interval and, although improved during the last three years, never became substantial.

In 1959, after failure of the original division manager to reduce indirect costs to levels desired by headquarters, the division was assigned a new manager. Indirect costs were promptly reduced. The sharpest reductions occurred in the marketing area where advertising was reduced by

DIVISION B		As Percentage of 1957				
	1957 base	1957	1958	1959	1960	1961
Gross sales billed	100	100	93	103	114	131
Direct costs	69*	100	90	95	110	130
Indirect costs	33*	100	81	88	93	90
Percent return on total gross assets**		−12	−3.9	1.3	0.4	1.9
Percent market share**		3.1	3.1	3.2	3.2	3.4

    * As percentage of GSB.
  ** Actual.

more than 50 per cent, division and regular sales by 10 per cent, and division order service, warehousing, and shipping by over 50 per cent. In 1961 the division was still operating its marketing activities at roughly the same expense level as was established after the 1959 cutbacks.

Gross sales billed in Division B rose almost steadily, and direct costs showed a corresponding increase. Indirect costs, however, were reduced. Again this leads to the prediction that earnings were unfavorable. Again the prediction is borne out by the division's record of return on total gross assets.

The largest reductions in indirect costs between 1957 and 1961 occurred in manufacturing and product development. This was largely due to the reduction in organization and other operating expense and customer order development. Marketing and administrative and general expenses experienced no marked changes over the period.

DIVISION C		As Percentage of 1957				
	1957 base	1957	1958	1959	1960	1961
Gross sales billed	100	100	83	106	84	84
Direct costs	62*	100	85	103	85	85
Indirect costs	26*	100	72	48	61	53
Percent return on total gross assets**		4.3	−5.7	20	10	20
Percent market share**		3.6	4.2	11	11	11

  * As percentage of GSB.
  ** Actual.

Gross sales billed in Division C have been somewhat irregular. Direct costs have moved almost proportionately with sales. Indirect costs, however, have been reduced much more than in proportion. This suggests that earnings in Division C have been unfavorable. In the first two years of the period this was certainly true. To correct this situation, a new division manager was installed in 1958. Indirect costs were promptly cut back in all areas, the most significant reductions occurring in manufacturing and product development.

The return on total gross assets rose sharply in 1959 as a result of improved sales and reduced indirect costs but fell again in the next year as sales dropped while indirect costs rose. The 20 per cent return was restored in 1961, however, through another cut in indirect costs.

Division D	As Percentage of 1957					
	1957 base	1957	1958	1959	1960	1961
Gross sales billed	100	100	103	115	192	274
Direct costs	68*	100	107	119	193	308
Indirect costs	25*	100	97	112	127	142
Percent return on total gross assets**		−5.6	−2.2	1.7	12	7.0
Percent market share**		4.2	4.2	4.5	6.6	8.3

    * As percentage of GSB.
    ** Actual.

Gross sales billed have risen steadily, indeed spectacularly, in Division D, while direct costs have risen more than in proportion. Although indirect costs also rose (and hence the situation does not completely satisfy the extremity conditions), the rise has been modest and is almost entirely explained as an increase in the "operating" class of indirect costs. Policy expenditures were held tightly in check. The prediction, therefore, is that earnings have been poor. Inspection of the return on the total gross assets record reveals that this is entirely correct.

Although increases in indirect costs occurred in all areas, the manufacturing increase was largely due to organization and other operating expense. A small increase occurred in product development engineering. In marketing the increase occurred mainly in division sales expense. Administrative and general expense also rose generally.

Division E	As Percentage of 1957					
	1957 base	1957	1958	1959	1960	1961
Gross sales billed	100	100	82	57	52	50
Direct costs	93*	100	80	52	47	44
Indirect costs	3.6*	100	108	167	167	212
Percent return on total gross assets**		46	48	44	39	38
Percent market share**		56	76	29	62	59

    *As percentage of GSB.
    **Actual.

Gross sales billed in Division E fell throughout the interval, and this was matched by corresponding reductions in direct costs. Indirect cost, however, rose sharply. Indeed, while sales and direct costs have been halved, indirect costs have doubled. This leads to the prediction that earnings must have been good to exceptional. And exceptional they were: average return on total gross assets over the period exceeded 40 per cent.

Increases in indirect costs occurred in all areas. Policy and operating classes shared the increases generally.

5.3.2. Apparent Contradictions

DIVISION F		As Percentage of 1957				
	1957 base	1957	1958	1959	1960	1961
Gross sales billed	100	100	78	67	78	70
Direct costs	57*	100	78	76	82	81
Indirect costs	15*	100	105	105	115	110
Percent return on total gross assets**		38	16	3.0	8.0	0.9
Percent market share**		27	24	25	24	26

* As percentage of GSB.
** Actual.

Gross sales billed in Division F fell almost continuously, and direct costs were reduced in the process. Indirect costs, however, increased, leading to the prediction that earnings had been good to excellent during the interval. Upon examination of the record of return on total gross assets the prediction is found to be incorrect. Although earnings had been excellent, they fell very sharply during the period and over the past three years were in the unfavorable range.

Upon further examination of Division F's record it was found that its history of exceptional earnings in 1957 goes back all the way through the 1950's. Thus for it to treat its indirect cost structure as institutionalized is entirely to be expected. In the face of persistent adversity of the sort that has been apparent since 1959, however, the continued failure of indirect costs to adjust to the new earnings record would constitute a contradiction of the model. As it turns out, Division F was reorganized in 1962 with the twin objective of reorienting its marketing strategy and reducing its indirect costs to acceptable levels. The contradiction, therefore, is apparent rather than real.

Division G		As Percentage of 1957				
	1957 base	1957	1958	1959	1960	1961
Gross sales billed	100	100	100	113	100	100
Direct costs	62*	100	103	107	105	107
Indirect costs	31*	100	94	109	107	107
Percent return on total gross assets**		−1.0	0.1	3.0	−3.1	−6.8
Percent market share**		9.8	9.4	9.5	9.3	8.5

*As percentage of GSB.
**Actual.

Gross sales billed in Division G have been exceptionally steady, while both direct costs and indirect costs have increased slightly. This leads to the prediction that earnings must have at least been fair. Upon inspection of the earnings record, the prediction is found to be incorrect.

A tentative explanation for this condition based on the changes in the composition of the indirect cost accounts was offered to the company's budgeting officials, and it turned out to be largely accurate. Thus, it was surmised that since the increases in indirect costs went entirely into improvements in plant facilities and product development while marketing and administrative staffs were actually reduced, plant and product must have been neglected in the earlier period. This was confirmed by the company budgeting officers who further stated that a new division manager had been assigned and that he had been given explicit instructions to correct this condition. Again, therefore, the contradiction is apparent rather than real.

5.3.3. Exceptional Performers. Of the following three divisions, two have shown fair and one has produced good earnings. Yet, despite steady or rising sales, none has significantly increased indirect costs as suggested by the verbal statement of the model. In each case the division management has been essentially unchanged over the interval so that presumably tastes have been the same throughout. Although they do not constitute contradictions of the "extreme" version of the hypothesis, their behavior is evidence that staff expansions do not inevitably accompany acceptable earnings reports.

Their performance records are shown below without comment.[13]

Division K	1957 base	As Percentage of 1957				
		1957	1958	1959	1960	1961
Gross sales billed	100	100	105	105	103	116
Direct costs	63*	100	100	100	100	113
Indirect costs	19*	100	108	108	108	117
Percent return on total gross assets**		26	26	27	26	30
Percent market share**		20	20	20	20	20

Division L	1957 base	As Percentage of 1957				
		1957	1958	1959	1960	1961
Gross sales billed	100	100	98	113	111	115
Direct costs	56*	100	98	111	110	113
Indirect costs	26*	100	90	107	107	100
Percent return on total gross assets**		11	12	15	14	14
Percent market share**		23	23	23	23	23

Division M	1957 base	As Percentage of 1957				
		1957	1958	1959	1960	1961
Gross sales billed	100	100	89	89	95	89
Direct costs	46*	100	88	83	83	83
Indirect costs	30*	100	91	91	100	91
Percent return on total gross assets**		14	11	12	14	11
Percent market share**		20	22	21	19	21

* As percentage of GSB.
** Actual.

[13] Rationalizations are easily provided. For example, the managements may have already provided themselves with as sizeable a staff as could reasonably be accommodated. It is also possible that the division managements have a comparatively low preference for staff. Possibly the stability of sales, earnings, and market share all contributed to a sense of security, thereby removing one of the incentives for expansion.

5.3. Evaluation. Interpreting behavior in the General Manufacturing Company was made difficult by their policy of decentralization and the diversity of the product line. Access to company documents and division records partly compensated for these difficulties. Of particular interest for purposes of evaluating the managerial discretion and entrepreneurial models are

1. The relationship of the headquarters unit to the operating divisions appears to be largely one where operating divisions are free to conduct their affairs without interference as long as they achieve a certain "objective" profit goal. This relationship is thus similar to the one that exists between the stockholders and the firm. There are, however, major differences that should be noted. First, the headquarters unit has access to vastly more information than the stockholders and hence is able to make a more exacting appraisal. Second, the machinery for replacing a division head is considerably simpler than that for replacing the company president. In both respects, the division is subject to greater pressure than is the firm. These conditions can be accommodated by a decentralized version of the managerial discretion model (see Section 3.4.3 of Chapter 8).

2. The discretionary character of residual funds was explicitly acknowledged in the company document describing expense planning. Earnings that exceed target performance are available for policy (i.e., discretionary) purposes. This is essentially how they are treated in the utility maximizing model.

3. The "model" that was submitted for comment to the top budgeting officials in the organization was, with minor qualifications, accepted as accurately reflecting gross characteristics of behavior. The tendency for staff activities to grow as long as profits permitted and the necessity to reduce staff when confronted by adversity were both acknowledged.[14] Both the tendency for the expansion of staff and the subsequent vulnerability of expanded staff during adversity are consistent with the managerial model.

4. The data on division performance are less detailed than the previ-

---

[14] In this connection, they pointed out the difficulty of imposing a profit constraint that exceeded "reasonable" levels. A division that exceeded a 15 to 20 per cent return on total gross assets effectively achieved autonomy and could successfully resist attempts to raise its profit goal.

ous studies. In general, however, they appear to reveal behavior that conforms to the verbal model and thus support the utility maximizing construction.

6. Some Observations from the Business Literature

Although the company studies are few in number, the list can be extended with ease. Examples of firms that respond to adversity in the way predicted by the discretion model are routinely reported in the business literature. *Fortune* has occasionally been concerned with the effect of adversity on business practices [125]. Almost any issue of *Forbes*, during a recession period, and frequently the *Wall Street Journal* will include a brief description of one or more leading firms making the kinds of adjustments that have been described. *Dun's Review and Modern Industry* has made this a survey topic with their President's Panel.[15] (The panel is composed of "nearly 200 leading corporation presidents ... [who] head manufacturing companies across the U.S.; with an average of 10,000 employees each and average annual sales of 188 million dollars") [48, p. 34].

Since the President's Panel survey was extensive, comparatively well-documented, and conducted in an atmosphere free from defensiveness, it provides a particularly relevant basis for evaluating the generality of the studies reported.

The *Dun's Review and Modern Industry* article begins with the following observation: "Prodded by sagging profits last year—and uncertainty about profits in 1961—corporations across the land are getting rid of *unproductive overhead* and trimming off deadweight" [48, p. 34] (italics added). This was not confined to only a few of the Panel members. "Formal cost reduction appears destined to assume a more important role in corporate activities during the next 12 months than during the past. Two-thirds of the Panel companies have already launched or are planning to launch formal [cost reduction] programs, as distinct from continuing review and controls" [48, p. 34]

The principles said to guide these cost reduction activities were (1) long-run effects must be given precedence over the short-run, (2) top management must supervise and itself make sacrifices in the cost reduction effort, (3) communications with the employees disclosing intent

---

[15] A recent issue of the *Wall Street Journal* also carried a survey on this matter [127].

must be maintained, (4) continuing, not just sporadic, cost control is essential [48, p. 36]. Yet in practice it is generally agreed that as profitability is restored, attention shifts away from cost control. Almost 90 per cent of the panelists agreed with the statement: "The incentives for careful policing begin to erode when the pinch eases. Cost-cutting programs must be closely policed to be effective" [48, p. 36].

Although within their own firms the production area was cited as the one most subject to pruning, in their estimates of the industry at large, the typical top executive found promotion and advertising as "the most promising cost-cutting targets, closely followed by the ever expanding area of administration and staff activities .... Production—the first cost-cutting choice at home—[was] picked by only 4 per cent as a worthy industry-wide target" [48, pp. 35–36]. Judging from the results of the studies reported in Sections 3–5, it would appear that the presidents' estimates of cost reduction opportunities among competitors are better indications of where costs can be cut in their own organizations. Their reports that production is the most fruitful area for cost reduction may reflect wishful thinking and thus be somewhat less than objective.

Although "big game is the long-range target of the cost cutter, ... the expense account ... still draws concentrated fire. A substantial number of Panel members are keeping close watch on all air travel .... A number of companies say they now take a harder look at participation in association meetings, out-of-state workshops, lectures, and conventions .... Another growing trend is toward closer review of expense statements" [48, p. 36].

The evidence appears to be roughly consistent with the discretion model. Thus the response of the firm to adversity is one where "everexpanding" staff is removed and emoluments disappear. The more severe the conditions, the more extensive the cuts. Although the profit maximization hypothesis also predicts that staff will be reduced in response to adversity, it is absolutely silent with regard to emoluments and quantitatively it may be difficult to reconcile the amounts of the cutbacks observed using a model constructed entirely around the profit maximization assumption—although this is made easier if a multi-period model with a minimum profit constraint is used (see Chapter 5, Section 1.2).

7. The Lump-Sum Tax: Allocation of Headquarters Expense as a Motivational Cost

The managerial discretion model predicts that the levy of a lump-sum tax causes the firm to reduce staff, output, and emoluments. The short-run profit maximization model predicts that the firm will be un-responsive to a lump-sum tax. The discounted profit maximization model also predicts that there will be no response unless the firm has encountered its minimum profit constraint, in which event staff and output are reduced. Although it is difficult to test this issue directly (lump-sum taxes are hard to come by), an indirect test is possible. The indirect test involves the allocation of headquarters expense to the operating divisions. The discretion model predicts that, since this reduces the earnings that the divisions show, and hence the amount of discretionary funds that they generate, it will cause them to adjust their decision variables so as to offset this effect—that is, to reduce staff, output, and emoluments and thereby increase actual profits reported.

This question was explored with the budgeting personnel in both the Midwest Processing Corporation and the General Manufacturing Company. No contact was made with anyone in Chemical Products Inc. who was intimately familiar with the accounting practices of the firm. In addition, the use of "profit centers" had not yet become important to its operations. As a result, the concept had no operational meaning in their organization.

7.1. Motivational Costs. The notion that cost information can be used motivationally has been advanced by Stedry [119]. He argues that individuals treat cost information not merely as objective data but also as stimuli. Hence, where the objective is to motivate efficient perform-ance, the appropriate data to provide may be data that have been systematically biased to produce the intended response. Although opera-tionally his model is not free from problems, a simplified version of it may prove eminently workable. Indeed, the use of a lump-sum tax to motivate performance is little more than a simple application of the Stedry costing principle. That is, by selectively introducing an opera-tional equivalent of a lump-sum tax into the accounting reports provided to operating personnel, behavior desirable to the parent organization may result.

7.2. General Manufacturing Company. The initial inquiry made to the officials of the General Manufacturing Company concern-ing the motivational use of costs was both direct and general. The ques-tion was: "Would it be possible to distort actual cost figures so as to encourage behavior that could not be obtained using actual cost figures?" The immediate response was one of alarm. This was followed by an explanation of why this would not be feasible. First, it was believed that the division managers had too intimate a knowledge of their own costs to permit such distortion. Second, any discovery of distortions would lead to very undesirable consequences. They did not, however, claim that improved performance was unattainable or that discreet use of the principle of motivational costs could not produce the desired results.

Using an indirect but more explicit question led to further insights on this issue. Thus to the question, "Would division managers react to an increase in their allocation of headquarters expense?" the response was more definite. Certainly they would react. Even so small an increase as 10 thousand dollars (in an allocation that was typically of the order of several hundred thousand dollars) would produce a vigorous response. This was documented by the experience of one of the headquarters budgeting personnel who had only recently returned from one of the divisions. He reported that the division manager, on being informed of a 10 thousand dollar increase in the allocation of headquarters overhead, insisted that this imposed an unfair burden on his division and made it difficult, if not impossible, for him to meet his profit goals. Yet, after his efforts to renegotiate were refused, he responded by looking for ways in which to absorb this amount in improved performance.

The rationale for distributing headquarters expense to the operating divisions was explored and elicited the following response:

1. Allocating headquarters expenditures to the divisions is necessary for product pricing. If these costs were not allocated, the divisions would price at levels that would fail to recover total corporate expenses.

2. Headquarters expenditures are partially recoverable on government cost-plus contracts and hence should be distributed.

3. Despite the fact that managers are told that they are responsible for costs only to the extent that these are subject to their own control, it is nonetheless clear, both to the division managers and among headquarters personnel, that an important criteria for performance is return on total gross assets, and this is computed *after* allocation on headquarters expenses. This is very explicit. "Return on investment [is] the primary measure of performance of [the] divisions. Income before taxes [but after allocation of headquarters expense] compared to gross assets is the ultimate measure of whether or not a division has met its objective." Hence, the distribution of headquarters expenses to the divisions affects the earnings they report and influences division costs indirectly

by making it all the more necessary that division expenses be kept under effective control.

The latter point is an implicit admission that not only can cost data be used motivationally but *they already are.* Indeed, expense control is the principal reason for distributing headquarters overhead to divisions that are neither able to influence price nor engaged in government contracts. This constitutes an indirect test of the prediction obtained from our model that levying a lump-sum tax would cause the firm to move its decision variables toward the profit maximizing position. For what is an allocation of headquarters expense other than an operational equivalent of a lump-sum tax?

Although at present the aggregate of the individual allocations to the divisions sums to the "actual," this is by no means a necessity. The knowledge of the "actual" figure can be easily controlled. Thus, it is possible to use this allocation more specifically in a motivational way.

7.3. Midwest Processing Corporation. The allocation of headquarters expense as a motivational cost was pursued at the Midwest Processing Corporation by asking the direct question, "Do allocations of headquarters expenses to the divisions influence their performance?" The answer was, "No, the divisions are responsible only for the costs they control." The question was then rephrased: "Would the divisions object to an assignment of additional headquarters expense?" This time the answer was "certainly." Asked to elaborate, the budgeting officer concerned indicated that spending on discretionary activities at the divisions was a function of division's profits and these were computed after allocation of headquarters expense. An increase in the amount of headquarters expense assigned to the divisions would require discretionary spending to be cut back.

Thus, although for the purposes of controlling materials and labor cost the allocation of nondivision expense is of no consequence, this allocation would affect spending for other activities—such as office improvements, expense accounts, and the level of staff expenditures. In conformance with the discretion model, a lump-sum tax (or its operational equivalent—allocation of headquarters expense) does appear to produce the predicted response.

7.4. Evaluation. The evidence is indirect that a lump-sum tax will produce the response predicted by the discretion model. However, an effort was made to put the question in a meaningful way. Thus the question was not, "How would a lump-sum tax affect your operations?" Instead, headquarters expense was used as the means for studying this problem. The responses obtained suggest that not only can headquarters expense be used to produce the response predicted by the managerial discretion model to a change in a lump-sum tax, but it already is used for this purpose.

8. Conclusion

The "extreme instance" occupies an important methodological position in the analysis. The choice of this device was motivated largely by the desire to avoid the *ceteris paribus* problem and thereby obtain reasonably sharp tests of the implications of the theory. It is well-suited for this purpose. It avoids both the necessity of providing a complete specification of the entire system as well as the confounding that is present when only moderate fluctuations occur along the dimensions of interest.

The field studies were concerned with the effect of adversity on firm behavior. Both the type and the magnitude of the responses observed as well as the descriptions of behavior from the company documents appear to be consistent with that predicted by the managerial discretion model. In addition, the observations produce insights into the ways that managers perceive their problems. For the most part they are cognizant of the types of nonprofit activities that go on in the organization and how these are related to the condition of the environment. By discriminating according to both "competitive pressure" and "individual management philosophy" in their efforts to reduce costs and adjust to adversity, they behave in a way consistent with the discretion model.

Reference to the business literature suggests that the field study reports, in a gross sense at least, are not without generality.

The evidence on the effect of a lump-sum tax is indirect and less extensive. Such as it is, it indicates that firms would respond in the way predicted by the managerial discretion model and that allocations of headquarters overhead may actually be used in this fashion presently.

CHAPTER 7

Principal Firm Analysis *

Whereas the previous chapter was concerned with studying the quantitative responses of the firm to adversity by use of the field study technique, the present chapter is concerned with examining "particular behavior" in the firm using statistical techniques. Tests of particular behavior are based on the proposition that opportunities for discretion and managerial tastes will have a decided impact on the expenditures of the firm. More precisely, those expenditures that promote managerial satisfactions should show a positive correlation with opportunities for discretion and tastes. The profit maximizing theory is somewhat ambiguous on this question. Interpreted as a theory in which the firm is operated entirely in the stockholders best interests, it clearly implies that expenditures which under the utility maximizing hypothesis will be positively correlated with measures of discretion and tastes, will instead be uncorrelated with these relationships. Interpreted somewhat more loosely, closer agreement with the utility maximizing hypothesis can be obtained. Thus, it is possible that the management first selects that physical combination of factors that maximizes profits and then absorbs some amount of actual profit as cost. These absorbtions may be correlated with the same measures of discretion and taste as would be expected under the utility maximizing theory. Hence, evidence that managers respond to opportunities for discretion is not inconsistent with the profit maximizing theory, but neither is evidence to the contrary; the theory is simply silent on this question. However, the failure of firms to respond

---

* The material reported in this chapter appeared in the December 1963 issue of *The American Economic Review*.

to opportunities for discretion constitutes a contradiction of the utility maximizing hypothesis, while observations that firms do display expense preference behavior supports it.

Since the evidence on expense preference behavior that is examined in this chapter does not bear on the effects of a staff component in the firm's utility function, the tests have direct relevance only for the emoluments version of the discretion models. That is, the evidence applies to the model $U = U[M, \pi - \pi_0 - T]$, rather than the combined staff-emoluments model. Indeed, those advocates of the profit maximizing theory who support the "loose" interpretation of it given above appear to be implicitly using this emoluments version of the discretion models.[1]

A general "expense preference" model designed to handle cross-section data is provided in Section 1. The effects of discretion and management tastes on executive compensation are examined in Section 2. The influence of tastes on retained earnings are studied in Section 3.

1. An Expense Preference Model

The history of the firm's profitability was used as a measure of the size of the firm's opportunity set in studying time-series behavior within a given firm in the previous chapter. For cross-section studies across firms and across industries, however, the differences that occur in accounting practices and performance standards suggest that the profit rate may not be a good measure of the size of this opportunity set. Instead, a measure of competition in the product market would be better suited to make these comparisons. In addition, an estimate of the effect of competition in the capital market and managerial tastes should be included. Thus if X is an expenditure for which a positive expense preference exists, I_1 is an index of the absence of competition, I_2 is an index of management taste, I_3 is an index of stockholder diffusion, and $f(\pi)$ is the level of X that would be supported solely by profit considerations, then under the utility maximization hypothesis

$$X = f(\pi)g(I_1, I_2, I_3)$$

where $\partial X/\partial I_i > 0$, all i. Under the stockholder version of the profit

---

[1] It will be recalled that the emoluments model in Chapter 4 preserved the marginal cost-benefit equalities of the traditional theory so that actual profit and maximum profit are identical. However, reported profit is less than actual by the amount of profit absorbed by expenditures on emoluments. This appears to conform to the "loose" interpretation of the profit maximizing hypothesis that is offered above.

maximization hypothesis, the partial derivative of X with respect to each of the I_i will be zero.

Since it is in the large corporation that manifestations of discretionary behavior are alleged to be important, and as complete data are most readily available among larger industrial firms than their smaller counterparts, the tests are restricted to those firms that clearly qualified as "principal firms." Among the 26 industries included in the analysis, selection was limited to the two largest firms, ranked according to sales, in each. The list of industries and firms included appears in Appendix 7-A. The tests performed are cross-section tests for the years 1953, 1957, and 1961. Thus they cover the period from the close of the Korean War to the present.

2. Executive Compensation

Stigler has observed that the estimation of the effect of monopoly on profit may be complicated by the absorption of some fraction of "true" monopoly profit as cost. In particular, "the magnitude of monopoly elements in wages, executive compensation, royalties, and rents is possibly quite large" [123, p. 35]. The evidence presented here is limited to testing only a part of this hypothesis. Specifically, I examine the effects of discretion on compensating the top executive.

Focusing on a single representative of management might appear to severely restrict the relevance of the results. If the compensation of the rest of the management group was determined independently of that of the chief executive, this would certainly be the case. However, payments between executive levels are carefully scaled [73, p. 320] [111]. Hence, the factors that influence compensation to the top executive can be presumed to affect the level of staff compensation generally.

Under the utility maximizing hypothesis, a positive expense preference toward emoluments exists. In particular, executive salaries should be correlated with the opportunities for discretion. Letting W_a be the actual salary of the management and W_c be the competitive salary, we have

$$W_a = W_c + (W_a - W_c)$$

where $W_a - W_c$ is a measure of the monopoly returns withdrawn by the management (by virtue of its advantageous position) as economic rent.

As indicated above, the hypothesis that discretion influences expenses takes the form

$$X = f(\pi)g(I_1, I_2, I_3)$$

where $f(\pi)$ is the expense incurred strictly on a profit maximizing basis and I_1, I_2, and I_3 are indices of the absence of competition, the tastes of the management, and the diffusion of the stockholders, respectively. Specifying $f(\pi)$ for purposes of studying executive compensation is somewhat difficult. A measure of hierarchical activity over which the executive in question has responsibility together with the special abilities required for the position probably measures this approximately. For the top executive, the level of hierarchical activity is effectively the entire staff structure. Thus, let $f(\pi) = f'(S, Z)$, where S is the level of staff (general administrative and selling expense)[2] and Z is an index of special ability.

It is assumed that the index of competitive pressure (I_1) is reflected by the concentration ratio and the entry barrier in each industry. The concentration ratio reflects the influence of realized interdependencies between rivals. Where concentration ratios are high, interdependencies will generally be intimate and behavior between rivals will at least be circumspect and may involve explicit agreements. In either case, the influence of competition will be consciously controlled. Hence, an increase in the concentration ratio will tend to widen the opportunities for managerial discretion. Obviously, this measure is defective and there will be exceptions. However, this will be true of almost any measure; all that is intended is to account for average rather than exceptional behavior.

---

[2] Previous studies of executive compensation have used the total revenue of the firm for this purpose [79] [96]. This has the advantage of minimizing errors of measurement that arise from differences in accounting practice but is probably not as good a proxy for "staff" as is general administrative and selling expense. Sales is defective for two reasons. For one thing, it reflects activity at levels below the management hierarchy, whereas the size effect would be expected to act largely within the hierarchy [111]. Secondly, interfirm comparisons are complicated by differences in vertical integration policies. As a matter of curiosity, regressions replacing general administrative and selling expense by sales were run, as well as regressions that included both of these variables. The results indicate that the sales variable has less power. The objections to using general administrative and selling expense as a proxy for hierarchical expense are largely related to differences in accounting practice among firms. However, the components of general administrative and selling expense very nearly give us a measure of the level of staff activity in the firm. Amounts charged to these accounts are, for the most part, current costs and hence ambiguities arising from the use of historical costs are reduced.

The barrier to entry measure, as developed by Bain [7], is explicitly designed to estimate the extent to which firms are insulated from the effects of competition. Although concentration and entry conditions are correlated, they are by no means identical. In combination they probably provide a particularly good measure of the opportunities for discretion. High concentration together with a high barrier to entry will tend to produce substantial discretion, for not only is potential competition limited but existing rivals are few enough to appreciate their conditions of interdependence. Low values for each of these measures will tend to produce the reverse effect, whereas mixed values, presumably, give rise to mixed effects.

To allay any suspicion that the concentration ratio and entry barriers are merely another measure of size, it might be noted that the product-moment correlations between the logarithm of sales and the logarithms of "staff," concentration, and barriers (for the firms included in the sample) are about 0.75, −0.13, and 0.15, respectively. Quite clearly these latter two correlations are small enough that if concentration and barriers have an effect on compensation, it is not primarily due to their relationship to size.

A sharp measure of managerial tastes (I_2) is not available. However, the composition of the board may act as a proxy measure of the extent to which management desires to operate the firm free from outside interference. Although low proportional representation of the management on the board of directors need not reflect a "taste" for active outside participation in the affairs of the firm, clearly a high internal representation does reflect the intent of the management to conduct the affairs of the firm free from such outside influence. It is hypothesized that as the management representation on the board increases, there tends to be a subordination of stockholder for managerial interests. In this sense, the composition of the board reflects management's attitude toward discretionary resource allocations, and a voluntary change in composition reflects a change in these "tastes."

The sources of the data for each of the above-mentioned variables are described in Appendix 7-B.

An estimate of stockholder diffusion (I_3) was not obtained. Such a measure would probably be correlated with the composition-of-the-board variable. However, the association may not be great. Where substantial concentration of ownership exists, there is frequently a tendency toward nepotism. This in turn may produce high internal representation rather than the high outside representation that would otherwise be predicted.[3]

---

[3] See, for example, the field study report on Chemical Products Inc. in Chapter 6.

If, in fact, the correlation were zero (and there were no other neglected variables to consider), the estimate of the "composition" effect would be unbiased. As it is, some bias may result from the lack of a diffusion measure.[4]

The effects of each of the independent variables on executive compensation should be positive. In addition, they are assumed to be multiplicative. Thus it is assumed that

$$(1) \qquad\qquad X_i = \alpha_0 S_i^{\alpha_1} C_i^{\alpha_2} H_i^{\alpha_3} B_i^{\alpha_4} U_i$$

where X_i = compensation of the top executive

S_i = general administrative and selling expense (i.e., "staff")

C_i = concentration ratio in the industry

H_i = height of the barrier to entry in the industry

B_i = composition of the board

U_i = a random error term[5]

and the subscript i refers to the ith firm in the sample.

Taking logarithms of both sides of the equation and using these data to obtain least-squares estimates of the net regression coefficients, the results shown in Table 1 are obtained.

The signs for each of the parameters in all three years are as predicted by the expense preference hypothesis. Moreover, with the exception of the composition of the board coefficient, which is significant at the 10 per cent level only in 1957, all of the regression coefficients are highly significant—two-thirds being significant at the 2.5 per cent level.[6] Whereas the relation of executive compensation to general administrative and selling expense (i.e., "staff") is almost certain to be positive and significant, it is not obvious that the measures of tastes and discretion that are introduced should have the effects shown (unless one endorses the view

---

[4] Alternatively, the composition-of-the-board variable might be interpreted as reflecting the *joint* effects of management's tastes and stockholder diffusion. What is really needed, however, are sharper measures that reflect each of these effects separately.

[5] U_i includes the effects of special abilities (the Z variable mentioned above), the omitted stockholder diffusion variable, numbers of years the top executive has held that position, and other neglected factors. The product of these factors is assumed to be uncorrelated with the independent variables in Equation 1.

[6] The tests are one-tailed tests, which are appropriate since the hypothesis specifies that the signs should be positive (which they are). The standard errors shown are corrected for the finite population correction $[(N - n)/N]^{1/2}$, where N is 100 in all years and n is 26, 30, and 25 for 1953, 1957, and 1961, respectively. See Appendix 7-A. Whether the results apply to a larger group than these 100 principal firms remains a subject for subsequent investigation.

TABLE 1. REGRESSION OF EXECUTIVE COMPENSATION ON "STAFF", CONCENTRATION
RATIO, COMPOSITION OF THE BOARD, AND BARRIERS TO ENTRY

	Year		
	1953	1957	1961
"Staff"			
Coeff.	0.228*	0.240*	0.218*
S.E.	0.061	0.052	0.054
Partial	(0.564)	(0.610)	(0.614)
Concentration			
Coeff.	0.503*	0.513*	0.422**
S.E.	0.157	0.143	0.152
Partial	(0.517)	(0.517)	(0.470)
Composition			
Coeff.	0.137	0.139	0.053
S.E.	0.118	0.101	0.120
Partial	(0.213)	(0.224)	(0.084)
Entry barriers			
Coeff.	0.446*	0.221**	0.200
S.E.	0.110	0.114	0.126
Partial	(0.606)	(0.307)	(0.290)
Coeff. of correl.			
(adjusted)	0.786	0.724	0.687

   * Significant at the 0.1 per cent level.
  ** Significant at the 2.5 per cent level.

that management responds to opportunities for discretion in the ways indicated). If, as suggested above, the compensation of the chief executive generalizes to the entire staff structure, these results have broad significance for the resource allocation process within the business firm. Furthermore, I would expect that these same measures of discretion would produce similar effects over the entire range of expenditures on perquisites (expense accounts, office services, and so forth).

Of course it could be argued that the concentration ratio and entry barrier variables have positive regression coefficients because they are correlated with the profit rate—that this profitability effect is responsible for the results obtained. But obviously the causality runs from concentration and entry barriers to profits rather than the reverse. Thus, by focusing on the market structure, the model directs attention to the ultimate determinants of discretionary behavior (competition in the product market) rather than the apparent determinant (the profit rate). Although these market variables might not perform as well as the profit rate among the smaller firms in the industry, it does not seem inappropriate to use them for studying the behavior of the two largest firms where the relationship between market structure and behavior is probably reasonably direct. Indeed, it is of interest to note that (1) if the profit rate on the stockholders equity is substituted for the concentration ratio and entry barrier variables, the coefficient of determination (R^2) falls to two-thirds of the value obtained using these market variables in 1953 and 1961, and yields less than a 10 per cent increase in R^2 in 1957; (2) if the profit rate, concentration ratio, and entry barrier variables are all included, the profit rate is significant only in 1957 and has the wrong sign in 1961, while the concentration ratio and entry barrier variables remain significant at the 10 per cent level or better in every year.

Although the profit rate might perform better if a weighted average were used instead of current values, the argument offered above, that this is an apparent rather than the ultimate determinant of behavior, still applies. Moreover, the appropriate estimate of the profit rate is the actual rather than the reported rate. But the actual rate is unknown if, as the evidence above suggests, some fraction of actual profits is absorbed as salary and perquisites.

Some feeling for the responsiveness of salary to the independent variables can be obtained by taking the median of the estimates for each parameter and finding the effect on salary of increasing each individual independent variable by a factor of two. In some gross sense, executive salaries will possibly increase on the order of 17 per cent if the level of staff activity were to double, on the order of 41 per cent if the concentration ratio in the industry were to double, on the order of 10 per cent if the internal representation on the board were to double (although this estimate is to be treated with considerable scepticism), and on the order of 25 per cent if the industry of which the firm was a part had a substantial or high barrier to entry rather than a low one. Thus, not only are the signs as predicted by the theory, but the magnitudes are sufficiently large to render somewhat doubtful the contention that discretionary effects are unimportant.

3. Earnings Retention

The composition-of-the-board variable was used in the executive compensation model to reflect the "tastes" of the management for discretion. Internal representation on the board is assumed to act as a proxy for the attitude of the management toward outside influence. As the proportional representation of management on the board increases, it is assumed that stockholder interests tend to be subordinated to managerial objectives. This was manifested in the executive compensation regression by the positive (although not significant) regression coefficient associated with the composition-of-board variable.

A second test for this effect is to examine the relationship between composition of the board and earnings retention policy. That is, how does management's "taste" influence the distribution of discretionary profit? Consistency with the argument above requires that the earnings retention ratio be directly related to the composition of the board. This follows since retained earnings are a source of discretion and a high internal representation provides the opportunity for management to shift the dividend policy to its advantage.

Alternative theories of the firm that regard managerial objectives as unimportant implicitly predict that there will be no association between the composition of the board and retention policy. Thus, the hypothesis of a positive association is tested against the null hypothesis of no association.

Earnings retention will, of course, be responsive to a number of considerations other than that of the composition of the board. Most important, investment opportunities will differ between industries and these could easily be overriding. If it can be assumed that the firms in the same industry have identical opportunities, however, these effects can be neutralized.

A paired comparison technique was used to neutralize the industry effects. That is, between the two principal firms in each of the 26 industries, the composition of the board and earnings retention ratio is compared. The random variable can take on either of two values: 1 if the higher internal representation is paired with the higher earnings retention ratio, and 0 otherwise. Hence, it is distributed as a binomial. Under the hypothesis that no association exists, the expected number of times the positive association will occur divided by the total number of observations is one-half. Thus the null hypothesis is that the binomial parameter p is 0.50. The alternative hypothesis is that the positive association will occur more than one-half of the time, i.e., that p exceeds 0.50.

The results for each of the three years as well as the pooled results for all three years are shown in Table 2.

The proposition that internal representation has no effect on the earnings retention policy between pairs of firms in the same industry is

TABLE 2. BINOMIAL TEST FOR ASSOCIATION BETWEEN COMPOSITION OF BOARD AND EARNINGS RETENTION POLICY

	1953	1957	1961	All Years
Number of observations	25	26	26	77
Expected number of positive occurrences under the null hypothesis	12.5 ($p = 0.50$)	13 ($p = 0.50$)	13 ($p = 0.50$)	38.5 ($p = 0.50$)
Actual number of positive occurrences	13.5 ($\hat{p} = 0.54$)	16 ($\hat{p} = 0.62$)	18 ($\hat{p} = 0.69$)	47.5 ($\hat{p} = 0.62$)
Probability that a value as high as observed would occur if the null hypothesis were true*	0.34	0.13	0.02	0.02

* Normal approximation to the binomial was used to obtain the probabilities that the null hypothesis would produce the results observed.

unsupported by the data. In every year the proportion of higher-higher observations exceeds 0.50. In 1953 and 1957 the probability that a value as high as that observed if the null hypothesis were true is 0.34 and 0.13, respectively, and in 1961 this drops to 0.02. Clearly, we are inclined to reject the hypothesis in favor of the suggested alternative. That is, due to the discretion that derives from the retention of earnings and the opportunity to influence the retention policy which arises from representation on the board, the positive association relation is supported by the data. Although it is possible that the composition of the board is acting only as an intervening variable and that the real explanation for this association lies elsewhere, no simple connection suggests itself.

The strongest evidence in favor of this hypothesis is provided by the pooled results for all three years. Here the observed number of positive occurrences would happen by chance under the null hypothesis with a probability of only 2 times in 100. Before the pooling of the observations can be justified, however, it is first necessary to establish that the observations are independent and that the association observed in one period is simply not carried over to the following period. Since the composition of the board and earnings retention decisions reflect policy considerations that exhibit continuation in consecutive years, lack of independence between consecutive years would be expected. On the other hand, the observations reported here are separated by a period of four years. The association between consecutive years may well be eliminated over this interval. Since the issue can scarcely be resolved on a priori grounds, the hypothesis that the observations are independent is submitted to test.

A chi-square test for association was used. A low value of χ^2 is consistent with the hypothesis that the observations between successive four-year intervals are independent. The value of χ^2 between 1953 and 1957 is 0.0065, and between 1957 and 1961 is 0.62. Sampling randomly from independent populations, values as high or higher than this would occur 95 per cent and 45 per cent of the time respectively. Hence the hypothesis of independence is supported,[7] the pooling of the observations is justified, and the best test for the composition-of-the-board effect is that of all three years combined. Here the possibility that the positive association observed has occurred by chance is only 0.02. Indeed, among pairs of principal firms it would appear that the firm with the higher internal representation on the board of directors will have a higher earnings retention ratio about three-fifths of the time.

The results above are limited to directional effects only and say nothing about the magnitudes involved. This is probably all that the data justify. However, a crude estimate of the quantitative effect is available by an application of the general model suggested above for studying discretionary expenditures. Thus let

R_{ik} = retained earnings ratio
ρ_k = the rate of return on investment available to principal firms
C_k = the concentration ratio
H_k = the entry barrier
B_{ik} = the composition of the board of directors
V_{ik} = a random error term[8]
and the subscript i refers to the firm and the subscript k refers to the industry of which the firm is a part.

Then, assuming that the relation is multiplicative, we have

$$(2) \qquad R_{ik} = \beta_0 [f(\rho_k)]^{\beta_1} C_k^{\beta_2} H_k^{\beta_3} B_{ik}^{\beta_4} V_{ik}$$

---

[7] This apparent independence suggests that a fluid situation in the relations between principal firms exists. It would be interesting to relate this to changes in top executive personnel or relative profitability to see if such factors as these are responsible.

[8] Neglected variables that may influence the retained earnings policy include liquidity measures (such as the current ratio), times interest earned, and other financial variables. Among principal firms in the same industry, such measures tend to display substantial stability.

Taking the ratio of retained earnings between the ith and jth principal firms in the same industry yields

(3)
$$\frac{R_{ik}}{R_{jk}} = \left(\frac{B_{ik}}{B_{jk}}\right)^{\beta_4} V'$$

Taking logarithms of both sides of the equation, the value of β_4 can be estimated by least squares. The resulting estimates for 1953, 1957, and 1961 are 0.17, 0.17, and 0.16, respectively, but only the 1957 estimate is significant at the 10 per cent level.[9] These estimates suggest that the retained earnings ratio would increase by about 12 per cent if the internal representation on the board of directors were to double.

A tenuous connection between the composition of the board and the investment policy of the firm can be obtained by noting the results obtained by Myron Gordon and M. Fg. Scott in their recent studies of investment financing. Thus Gordon remarks that, "The really surprising result is produced by return on investment .... In both industries there is a statistically significant tendency for the retention rate to fall as the corporation's rate of return increases. We must conclude that either [our estimate] is a poor measure of rate of return on investment or that corporations are not primarily influenced by the price of their stock in setting dividend rates" [53, pp. 231–32]. And Scott, in a somewhat more broadly based study of dividend policy, observes that the "negative correlation of -0.30 between undistributed profits ... and the subsequent growth of earnings ... is somewhat surprising. It suggests that stockholders ... might benefit from more generous dividend distributions" [106, p. 244]. For a theory that makes the firm's objectives identical with those of the stockholders, such a result is somewhat disquieting. For an approach that permits the subordination of stockholder to managerial objectives, however, a possible explanation for these results can be provided by tying them into the composition of the board analysis above.

As was suggested above, high internal representation on the board of directors favors attention to managerial objectives, and this is manifested in a high earnings retention rate. The funds thus provided are available to the management for the pursuit of selective expansionary

---

[9] Since the estimates are sensitive to extreme values of retained earnings (values of R_{ik} greater than 0.95 or less than 0.05), and since such extreme values ordinarily represent a transitory condition, these extreme values were removed in making the estimates. Thus the estimated values of β_4 apply to the range of retained earnings between 5 and 95 per cent.

objectives. The resulting investment, being based on a combination of profit and expansionary goals, will exceed the amount dictated by profit considerations alone. As a result, the average rate of return in firms whose management is inclined to subordinate stockholder objectives can be expected to fall below that in firms where management interests are more nearly those of the stockholders.[10]

Thus the tastes of the management, as revealed originally in the composition of the board, make their influence felt through the earnings retention policy and thence on the return on investment. Where these tastes favor expansion, an adverse effect on the rate of return on investment results. This indirect implication of the utility maximization theory is precisely the result that Gordon and Scott report. Although conjectural, it suggests the value of including a "taste" variable, of which the composition of the board is a somewhat imperfect proxy, in future studies of the investment decision.

---

[10] In addition to the quantity of funds invested and diminishing rate of return effect, there may also be political influences to consider [38, Chap. 4]. As the amount of available resources increases, the importance of political relative to economic criteria will tend to increase. Any such a shift toward political considerations could be expected to have an adverse effect on the rate of return on investment.

Firms and Industries Included in the Analysis

Industry and Principal Firms*	1953	1957	1961
Aircraft			
Boeing			
General Dynamics			
Aluminum			
Aluminum Co. of America			
Reynolds			
Automobiles			
General Motors	x	x	x
Ford		x	x
Building materials			
Armstrong Cork			
Johns-Manville			
Chemicals			
Du Pont			
Union Carbide			
Computers and office machinery			
International Business Machines	x	x	x
Remington Rand	x	x	x
Containers			
American Can	x	x	x
Continental Can	x	x	x
Copper			
Anaconda			
American Smelting and Refining		x	x
(Phelps Dodge)	x	x	
Dairy products			
National Dairy			
Bordens			
Distilled liquor			
National Distilleries	x	x	x
Schenley		x	x
Electrical appliances and equipment			
General Electric			
Westinghouse Electric			

Industry and Principal Firms*	1953	1957	1961
Ethical drugs			
Pfizer (Chas.)			
Sterling Drug			
Farm and construction machinery			
International Harvester	x	x	x
Caterpillar Tractor	x	x	x
Flour milling and cereal			
General Mills	x	x	x
The Pillsbury Company	x	x	
Glass			
Pittsburgh Plate Glass			
Libbey-Owens-Ford			
Gypsum products			
U. S. Gypsum	x	x	x
National Gypsum		x	
Meatpacking			
Swift	x	x	x
Armour	x	x	
Packaged foods			
General Foods			
Standard Brands			
Paper and paperboard			
International Paper			
Crown Zellerbach			
Petroleum (International)			
Standard Oil of New Jersey	x	x	x
Socony Vacuum	x	x	x
Soap and toiletries			
Proctor and Gamble	x	x	x
Colgate Palmolive	x	x	x
Soft drinks			
Coca Cola			
Pepsi Cola			
Steel			
U. S. Steel	x	x	x
Bethlehem Steel	x	x	x
Textiles			
Burlington Industries	x	x	x
J. P. Stevens	x	x	
Tire and rubber			
Goodyear	x	x	x
Firestone	x	x	x

Industry and Principal Firms*	1953	1957	1961
Tobacco			
R. J. Reynolds	x	x	x
American Tobacco	x	x	x
Total of x's	26	30	25

* Firms within each industry grouping are the two largest firms according to 1957 sales. The paired comparison of the composition of the board with earnings retention was performed across all of the industries in each of the years with the exception of automobiles in 1953, when Ford was still a privately held corporation. The "x's" indicate firms and years for which complete data were available for the top executive compensation regression. Since data on Anaconda Company were incomplete in all three years, data on Phelps Dodge, the fourth largest copper company in 1957 and for which data were reasonably complete, was used in the regression.

The industries represent a sample of what might be called "major industries." The results reported presumably carry over to a somewhat broader population of major industries. Defining this population is somewhat arbitrary; Moody's listing of major industries perhaps is as satisfactory as any [87, pp. a16–a17]. On this basis, the following manufacturing industries would be added to the list above: air conditioning, automotive equipment, cement, controls and instruments, cosmetics, proprietary drugs, electronics, food-baking, food-biscuits, food-canning, lumber and wood products, machine tools, machinery and equipment, nonferrous metals (misc.), oil-integrated, oil-producing, oil-refining, photographic equipment, railroad equipment, rayon, shoes, TV-radio, and vending machines. This list of 24 industries added to the 26 industries given above yields a "population" of 50 major industries and, with 2 "principal firms" in each, a total of 100 principal firms.

APPENDIX 7–B

Sources of the Data

Executive Compensation: As a matter of law, publicly held corporations are required to report executive compensation to the Securities and Exchange Commission. Although these data are a matter of public record, they are not readily available. *Business Week*, however, annually publishes executive compensation figures for a group of principal firms. It was from this source that the data on compensation were obtained.

General Administrative and Selling Expense and Composition of the Board: Both were obtained from *Moody's Industrials*—although the composition of the board estimate was corrected occasionally when the listing of officers in *Moody's* was incomplete. Although the composition of the board effects come in somewhat weakly, it might be noted that out of the variety of possible ways to introduce this variable (as a dummy, weighted average, etc.), only the actual, current-period values were used. In subsequent investigations, some of these other variations will be explored.

Concentration Ratios: Data on concentration for 1953 were developed from the 1954 concentration ratios for the four largest firms reported in *Concentration in American Industry* (Washington, D.C., 1957). Concentration data for 1957 and 1961 were developed from the 1958 concentration ratios for the four largest firms reported in *Concentration Ratios in Manufacturing Industry 1958, Part I* (Washington, D.C., 1962). A weighted average of several of the SIC industry groups was sometimes used to arrive at a concentration ratio for the industries in question. Although such weighting procedures can produce distortions, they are probably not too serious in reasonably narrowly defined industry groups.

Barrier to Entry: Bain's study [7] provided the estimates of the height of the barrier to entry. In addition, I took the liberty of classifying textiles as an industry with a low entry barrier, since Bain did not include textiles in his analysis but there is general agreement that the industry has a low entry barrier. A dummy variable which took on the value 1 (ln 1 = 0) when the barrier to entry was low and e (ln e = 1) when the barrier was high or substantial was used in the regressions. Use of two dummy variables to represent the substantial and high entry conditions separately was also tried. Although one might suppose that the parameter for the high barrier dummy would exceed that of the substantial barrier dummy, the results were somewhat mixed. As I have suggested elsewhere, however, the principal difference between a substantial and high barrier may be that in the former case the firm expands selling expense beyond its optimal level in order to discourage entry, with the result that the effective condition of entry is approximately the same in substantial and high barrier industries [128]. The question requires additional empirical investigation.

CHAPTER 8

Social Choice in an Institutional Context

In what I have called the "entrepreneurial" version of the theory of the firm, the question of imputing a single-valued objective function to the firm is not even raised. The discretion which modern management has in directing the affairs of the firm is either absorbed in the person of a profit maximizing entrepreneur (a dictatorship assumption), or it is held to be unimportant to the theory of the firm since the managers will voluntarily choose to operate the firm in a profit maximizing fashion anyway (a unanimity assumption). In the first instance no problem in social choice is encountered since the firm is directed entirely by one individual. In the second instance the question of resolving differences is avoided by introducing unanimity; all of the managers uniformly desire to see the firm operated so as to maximize profit. Due largely to these strong assumptions, the theory provides strong predictions about how the firm will respond to changes in the data. Although descriptively false in detail, the assumptions may nevertheless be sufficiently accurate to permit the theory to handle a large class of circumstances of interest to economics.

The social choice question could also be disposed of under the utility maximizing hypothesis proposed by adopting either of these devices. Moreover, since it is largely on its predictions, rather than its assumptions, that this model will be evaluated, neglect of the social choice question would be somewhat defensible. Nevertheless, assumptions are relevant to the evaluation of a theory [39] [62]; it is thus of interest to examine the social choice question to determine the extent to which departures from dictatorship or unanimity can be permitted and still preserve the main results. The subsequent analysis will largely be directed to this objective. The social choice problem as posed by Arrow is stated in Section 1. This is followed by an examination of its relevance to institutional decision making in Section 2. The social choice question in the context of the theory of the firm is then developed in Section 3.

1. Arrow's General Possibility Theorem

The problem of specifying a value-free social welfare maximum has been of long-standing concern to economists. The New Welfare Economics was designed to achieve this objective.[1] However, as Bergson showed, no such value-free specification is possible [17]; the implicit value judgment of the New Welfare Economics was one of consumer sovereignty.

The fact that a value judgment (such as consumer sovereignty) is necessary in order to define the social optimum should neither be surprising nor, indeed, distressing. Were this the only problem, welfare economics would be in little trouble. Unfortunately, however, it is not. For one thing, there are a host of technical complications such as production and consumption externalities, the treatment of uncertainty, and planning horizons.[2] But even more devastating has been Arrow's demonstration that it is impossible to obtain a Social Welfare Function that satisfies a set of what appear to be generally desirable social choice properties.

Thus consider the so-called "paradox of voting." Suppose that in a three person community choice among alternatives A, B, and C the following preferences are indicated:

Individual 1: $A > B > C$

Individual 2: $B > C > A$

Individual 3: $C > A > B$

By inspection we see that a majority prefer A to B and a majority prefer B to C. If the community preference scale is defined to be one where the ranking of the majority determines the collective preference, we may then say that the community prefers A to B and B to C. Moreover, if community preferences are transitive, A will be preferred to C. But a

---

[1] The "compensation-principle" played a central role in this literature. See [64] [68].

[2] See [56] for a comprehensive statement of these and other technical problems.

majority prefers C to A. Thus preferences are intransitive and this method of aggregating individual preferences fails to satisfy an elementary condition of rationality. With this example Arrow then goes on to pose the crucial question, "Can we find other methods of aggregating individual tastes which imply rational behavior on the part of the community and which will be satisfactory in other ways?" [5, p. 3.]

In order to examine this issue Arrow sets up as initial conditions that individual choice conform to two axioms (complete ordering and transitivity) and that the social welfare function possess five properties. These properties may be characterized as (1) universal domain, (2) positive association of social and individual values, (3) independence of irrelevant alternatives, (4) citizens' sovereignty, and (5) nondictatorship.[3] If the axioms and conditions are all to be satisfied *and* if the possibility of interpersonal comparisons of utility is excluded, Arrow proceeds to show that, "*the only methods of passing from individual tastes to social preferences which will be satisfactory and which will be defined for a wide range of sets of individual orderings are either imposed or dictatorial*" [5, p. 59]. In other words, if interpersonal comparisons are disallowed, if individual preferences are to count, and if the "free triple" condition is to be maintained (which assures that a wide range of orderings are admissable), a consistent social welfare function cannot be devised. Efforts to cope with this result have moved in either of two directions: permitting interpersonal comparisons or relaxing one or more of Arrow's five conditions.

2. Relevance of the General Possibility Theorem to Social Choice Institutionally Conceived

2.1. The Paradox of Voting Reconsidered. It was seen that in the ordering of three things by three people that use of a majority voting rule for obtaining the community preference could lead to social intransitivity. That such a strong result could be obtained from this simple case would seem to condemn to failure any attempt to handle the community preference question. It is of some interest, however, to examine this result in somewhat more detail.

Thus, consider all possible orderings of three things by three people. Of the 216 possible orderings, intransitivities occur in only 12 cases. Hence, even if each possible ordering were equi-probable, a majority

---

[3] Since these conditions are developed in a large number of readily accessible references, it seems unnecessary to detail them here. See [5] [78] [98].

voting rule would produce socially transitive orderings almost 95 per cent of the time. And if the condition of maximum dissimilarity is eliminated (which is precisely the case considered in the "paradox"), transitive social orderings are obtained every time. Hence, if Arrow's first condition were removed—that is, if we were to restrict the domain and consider only preference profiles believed to be relevant rather than all possible orderings (as is required by the condition of universal domain)— the "paradox" disappears.

2.2. The Requisites of Institutional Viability. In his closing comments, Arrow suggests that by invoking certain institutional considerations, the social choice problem is less serious than his general analysis indicates. Thus, he observes,

> Individuals prefer certain political structures over others, not only because of their liking for the structure as such, but also because they have some idea of the preference patterns of other individuals in the society and feel on the whole they can expect the particular structure in question, taken in conjunction with the expected behavior of other individuals under that structure, to yield decisions on current matters which will usually be acceptable to themselves. Thus we may expect that social welfare judgments can usually be made where there is both a widespread agreement on the *decision process* and a widespread agreement on the *desirability* of everyday decisions [5, pp. 90–91]. (Italics added.)

That is, the membership in an organization will support the existing procedures for obtaining decisions and conform to the decisions that it renders as long as the mechanism operates acceptably. Although the decision-making process might possess defects, this need not produce an effort for reform. Frequent tinkering, it might be feared, could lead to conditions of instability which would endanger the entire system.[4] Should the decisions rendered become grossly unsatisfactory, of course, an active effort for change would enjoy considerable support and a change in the prevailing rules would be expected. With this exception, however, the attachment to the decision-making processes may provide a stable basis

---

[4] Thus an individual who has an aversion to "hot rods" might prefer to permit their continued existence rather than support legislation for their abolition. For if they are legislated away, what next? Perhaps the rose bushes which he enjoys but are responsible for his neighbor's allergy. In a more general sense, the preference against tinkering is reflected by those economists who prefer rules to authority.

for obtaining acceptable group preferences even in the absence of a highly articulated value consensus on issues submitted for determination.

Probably more important than this inertial attitude toward change in the decision-making machinery, however, are the processes for obtaining a value consensus that result from social interaction among the members of the group. In *ad hoc* groups, of course, this social conditioning may be very limited. But

> ... in contrast to the *ad hoc* group, the members of the established group have internalized the responses of the other members. Under these conditions it is to be expected that the performance of the establishing group on a problem-solving task will exhibit considerable similarity to the independent individual performance of the constituent members if the task is similar to ones carried out in the normal course of the activities of the established group [26, p. 175].

This is particularly true in institutional settings where potential members are screened by existing members before admission is granted. Where this is required, the new membership will ordinarily enter with a core of values common to that of the group, and the process of social conditioning will tend to produce an even closer identity. Indeed, if the social psychologists are correct in claiming that effective group maintenance requires the establishment of cohesiveness on basic issues [47], then a substantial value consensus becomes a necessary condition for a group's continued existence.

If, therefore, an agreement on the decision process and a value consensus on matters of policy are essential to the viability of groups, the dilemma posed by Arrow's result is largely irrelevant to social choice problems in many institutional contexts. In the "paradox of voting," for example, agreement on the majority voting procedure together with a modest value consensus among the group members would almost certainly provide a social choice function that yields both transitivity and complete ordering. For individuals selected at random, of course, such a result might not obtain. But in an *on-going group*, this is most unlikely.[5]

---

[5] Graaff would apply this argument more generally. Thus he suggests that, "However important intransitivity may be as a logical possibility, or as a theoretical virtue of democracy, in which it provides a safeguard against the consistent abuse of majority power, it is probably less important as a matter of fact. That is because, if a society is to cohere at all, let alone function as a political unit, its members must in some measure share a common ethic. Markedly different rankings of alternative choices must not occur too frequently. And the more nearly rankings coincide, the smaller the danger of intransitivity becomes" [57, p. 295].

2.3. Relevance, Power, and Consistency.

2.3. Relevance, Power, and Consistency. Rothenberg has argued that the three characteristics desirable in a social welfare function are relevance, power, and consistency [98, p. 301]. Relevance requires that the function reflect the prevailing values of the group. Power is a measure of the range of social choice situations upon which the function renders a social ordering. Consistency, essentially, requires transitivity among choices. Arrow's result demonstrates that not all three of these properties can be completely realized. However, not infrequently in positive economics (and sometimes in welfare economics) a compromise among criteria is necessary. A compromise is proposed here. Thus, it is proposed that by confining the analysis to well-defined institutional situations (that is, by sacrificing power and restricting the domain), that relevant, consistent social choice functions are often attainable. It is the force of the argument above that the commitment to the decision process and the existence of a value consensus provide the foundation for handling the social choice problem in such an institutional context.

2.4. Marschak on Social Choice.

2.4. Marschak on Social Choice. Marschak's statement of the conditions to be satisfied for a group to be a team, foundation, or coalition [82] is particularly appropriate since (1) he is expressly concerned with the social choice problem, (2) his assumptions are explicit, and (3) it is clear that to satisfy the assumptions for even the weakest group that he considers requires a restriction of the domain.

In Marschak's notation, the relation SG_iS' is read: from the standpoint of individual i, the state S is preferred or indifferent to the state S' (i.e., G_i is a weak ordering relation). The paired relations, G_i, $i = 1$, 2, ..., n denote individual orderings and G_0 the group ordering (if it exists). Let Σ denote the set of all states. In addition to the assumption of individual rationality, Marschak introduces the following conditions:

A. There exists a transitive ordering G_0 on Σ. [Thus *if SG_0S' and $S'G_0S''$ then SG_0S''*—but this does not assure that the group *can* order S, S', or S''.] *Transitivity of Group Interests.*

B. For any S, S', in Σ, if SG_iS' for all $i = 1, 2, ..., n$, then SG_0S'. *Pareto Optimality Principle.*

C. For any S, S' in Σ, SG_0S' or $S'G_0S$. [For no pair of states is it impossible for a group ordering to be assigned.] *Completeness of Group Preferences.*

D. For all $i = 1, 2, ..., n$, SG_iS' if and only if SG_0S'. [All individuals have identical interests.] *Unanimity.*

Marschak then defines the following groups:

If A and B are satisfied the group is a *coalition*.
If A, B, and C are satisfied the group is a *foundation*.
If A, B, C, and D are satisfied the group is a *team*.

Since all of his groups require assumption A, none is general enough to satisfy the conditions that Arrow requires in his proof of the General Possibility Theorem. That is, assumption A requires that where group preferences exist, they are transitive. But, as the discussion of the "paradox of voting" revealed, this can be true only if those cases of maximum dissimilarity of individual preferences are excluded. Implicity, therefore, Marschak is restricting the domain. Although this is easily overlooked (the conditions for a coalition seem quite innocuous), strict adherence to the Arrow conditions would prohibit use of any of these groups to analyze social choice questions.

By introducing individual numerical utility functions U_i, $i = 1$, 2, $\ldots$, n, on Σ Marschak redefines his groups in utility terms. If the group utility function U_0 is numerical then $U_0(S) > U_0(S')$ if and only if SG_0S'. In the case of *coalitions*, $U_0(S)$ is a vector $[U_1(S), \ldots, U_n(S)]$ (and vectors can be partially but not completely ordered).[6] In the case of *foundations*, $U_0(S)$ is numerical and a monotone non-decreasing function of $U_1(S)$, $U_2(S)$, $\ldots$, $U_n(S)$. For *teams*, $U_0(S) = U_1(S) = U_2(S) = \ldots = U_n(S)$. Whereas for a coalition the states can be partially ordered and Pareto optimality is satisfied, for a foundation they can be completely ordered, and for a team the group possesses unanimity.

Marschak finds it necessary to employ the unanimity assumptions to develop his "theory of teams." Since this is an extreme condition, it is difficult to justify on grounds of reasonableness. Groups may possess striking uniformities—but unanimity is somewhat severe. Yet, if it produces insights that cannot easily (if at all) be obtained using weaker assumptions, it fulfills a useful function and is likely to be considered acceptable.

The assumptions necessary to satisfy the conditions for a foundation are substantially weaker. Unanimity is no longer required, since the group need only possess a mechanism for completely ordering the states of the world. This requires agreement on the decision process (in effect, how individual preferences are to be weighted) as well as comparability

---

[6] If U_0 is a vector, $U_0(S) > U_0(S')$ if and only if $U_i(S) \geq U_i(S')$ for all i and $U_i(S) > U_i(S')$ for at least one i.

between individual utilities. Quite obviously, a value consensus will facilitate the making of such comparisons.

The conditions for a coalition are more general, but they may frequently fail to render a discrimination. Groups for which only the coalition assumptions are satisfied are apt to be loosely structured and ones for which a substantial value consensus is unnecessary to their continued existence.

2.5. Cardinal Utility. Cardinal utility was widely used by economists until it became evident that for most of the purposes for which cardinality had seemed essential, equivalent results would be obtained using ordinal assumptions. Where interpersonal comparisons are to be made, however, cardinality is usually required.[7] This usually takes the form of a Marshall-Jevons or a Von Neumann-Morgenstern utility function. In the former case, preferences are obtained by ranking differences. In the latter, risk choices are involved.[8] Whether these two would produce identical valuations of each of the relevant states of the world is an empirical question that has not been resolved. Rather than become involved in this controversy, it seems easier to follow Bridgeman's dictum for dealing with phenomena within the operating domain [25, p. 10]. Thus, where choice among certain prospects is involved, the Marshall-Jevons construction is appropriate; in risk choice situations the Von Neumann-Morgenstern approach can be used. In each case, individual cardinal utility functions unique up to a linear transformation are obtained. By using the value consensus to introduce appropriate bounds on the individual functions together with agreement on the decision process (weighting device), interpersonal comparisons of utility can be

---

[7] An exception is the single-peakedness condition proposed by Black [19]. It requires that there be at least one arrangement of the available alternatives such that each individual's preference among the alternatives can be plotted as a curve possessing a single peak. Thus an ordering will be single-peaked if, for some arrangement of the alternatives along the abscissa and the preference order along the ordinate, none of the preference curves includes a reversal. Single peakedness of course violates the condition of universal domain but, when it exists, the majority voting rule gives rise to selection of the median among the peak alternatives and the ordering will be transitive.

For the most part it seems to be a formalism which possesses desirable properties but, unfortunately, is too specialized to be of significant relevance to the question of social choice.

[8] See [45] for a description of the approach taken by each and a comparison of their properties.

made.[9] That is, for any group able to specify a complete ordering (Marschak's foundation), a cardinal utility measure that achieves inter-personal comparability should be empirically discoverable. For less-well-defined groups, this might not be possible. Indeed, efforts to obtain interpersonal comparability at a "general" level have not been notably successful.[10]

3. Social Choice in the Business Firm

The preceding discussion has emphasized that a value consensus is necessary to group maintenance. Agreement on this is substantial. The objective now is to examine (1) the necessity for a value consensus in the business firm, (2) the process by which the value consensus is obtained, and (3) the general effects. This completed, the implications of the argument will be examined in the context of the managerial discretion model.

3.1. The Necessity for Consensus. Barnard has indicated that "social compatibility" is an essential condition of employment—both to the individual and to the group with whom he works [9, pp. 146–49]. Indeed, he claims, this condition is neglected only at the risk of disruption. "Men often will not work at all, and will rarely work well, ... if the social situation *from their point of view* is unsatisfactory" [9, p. 147]. Lack of compatibility tends to inhibit communication through formal channels, and the informal channels may breakdown completely. Since effective communication is essential to organizational performance, the prior need of compatibility is evident.

In a field study of organizational effectiveness, Katz found that shared values among the president and the top executives facilitated collaboration. A value consensus existed both with respect to corporate goals and organizational procedures [70]. Similarly, Dibble reports that "higher ranking occupations are more likely than lower ranking occupations to have highly developed ideologies" [40, p. 231–32]. Such observations concerning the importance and existence of organizational compatibility and uniformity suggest that consensus within the policy-

---

[9] For an approach that weights the individual preferences equally, see [124].
[10] See [78] or [98]. The approach used in [124] makes the value judgment that preferences are to count equally.

making unit of the business firm is a necessary condition for long-run organizational viability.

3.2. The Process for Obtaining Consensus. The value consensus in the business firm is due to the combined effects of a screening-selection procedure with a socialization process. The former tends to provide members to the firm with compatible characteristics, the latter is a process by which the major values of the groups are internalized by its individual members [94, pp. 125, 135].

The screening-selection process occurs at several levels and at each it is usually a reciprocal one. It can be categorized by what Cyert and March have called "mating search," i.e., as one where the organizational unit is searching the environment for individuals who meet its needs while at the same time individuals are presenting their credentials for consideration [38, p. 80]. Since both the organizational unit and the individuals seeking employment use certain well-defined criteria to make the search efficient, a preliminary screening on both sides of this exchange takes place that tends to ensure that the alternatives considered will meet some advance standards of acceptability.

Once contact between the organization and the individual is established, a further evaluation occurs and a compatibility decision is reached by each. For the organization, the crucial questions are the compatibility and loyalty of the newcomers as evaluated by the existing management team [126, p. 98]. If employment arrangements are agreed upon, the individual then becomes part of and subject to the socialization process mentioned earlier. If he responds well to this process (both from the standpoint of the organization as well as that of the individual), continued employment is likely and promotion prospects may present themselves. At each stage up the promotion ladder, the bilateral screening selection process is repeated. Hence, at the very top, what may be very nearly a representative value system appears.

Barnard has explained this process in the following terms:

> The general method of maintaining an informal executive organization is so to operate and to select and promote executives that a general condition of compatibility of personnel is maintained. Perhaps often and certainly occasionally men cannot be promoted or selected, or even must be relieved, because they cannot function, because they "do not fit," where there is no question of formal competence [9, p. 224].

3.3. The Effects of Consensus. The group maintenance needs and processes in the business firm are almost certain to produce a leadership situation that can be characterized either as a benevolent dictatorship or as a committee system. In either case the effect is one where decisions are made in a fashion that reflect collective preferences.

Thus Cole has suggested that

> ... the term "entrepreneur" may be construed occasionally in the singular, but usually in the plural—and for two reasons. The first is that decision-making is the critical or key operation in entrepreneurship, and even in single-man proprietorships the head of the enterprise rarely decides by himself ... [without] the original suggestion or some later advice ... [coming] from subordinates or staff .... The second reason is that frequently nowadays decision-making in companies is purposefully plural. A president may exist, but he is only one among equals [32, p. 10].

And Gordon has observed that "the prevalence of group, instead of individual, action is a striking characteristic of management organization in the large corporation. In many cases, committees of executives have partially supplanted individuals in the formulation and approach of major decisions, and they frequently share with the chief executive the exercise of the final coordinating function" [54, p. 94]. Indeed, with respect to the policy-making machinery generally, "the ... rule is that corporate executives as a group determine the volume and direction of investment in their firms; they set prices and formulate price policies; and, in general, they make the important decisions which constitute the heart of what many economists call the entrepreneurial function" [54, p. 114].

3.4. Social Choice and the Managerial Discretion Model. The social choice question as it applies to the managerial discretion model can be viewed from three vantage points. The first that will be considered is that of benevolent dictatorship. A more general result can be obtained by using Marschak's foundation assumptions. Finally, the effect of decentralization on social choice is examined.

3.4.1. Benevolent Dictatorship. It is important to distinguish benevolent dictatorship from the dictatorship assumption invoked in the entrepreneurial model. The latter might better be referred to as "autocratic dictatorship" so as to better reflect the intent that it represents only the value system of the entrepreneur (or owner), and that all the other employees in the organization take an oath of fealty to his value system as a condition of employment. Benevolent dictatorship is a less severe assumption in that it makes allowance for the social processes in the organization and the needs of the employees. In a sense, the notion of a benevolent dictator is close to what Papandreou appeared to mean by his "peak coordinator." Thus, the preference system accepted by the peak coordinator is, according to Papandreou, "a resultant of all the influences which affect the value premises of enterprise strategy selection" [92, p. 204].[11]

That the head of an organization is empowered to hire and fire his subordinates and to approve or reject their proposals does not imply that it is only his values that influence his choices. For although he possesses all of the formal power to run the organization as he sees fit, he must, if he is to have a viable organization for long, give consideration to the values of those in close association with him and upon whom he must depend to have the affairs of the organization effectively attended to. Thus, despite *apparent* dictatorship power, the head of an organization finds himself subject to certain organizational phenomena which require him, even if he should wish otherwise, to select his strategies subject to constraints—from a subset acceptable to his associates rather than from the whole space.

This viewpoint is implicit in the "theory of authority" proposed by Barnard [9, Chapter 12] and developed by Simon [113, Chapter 7]. Thus they emphasize that the subordinate rather than the superior determines the area of acceptance and hence the scope of authority. In a free society, particularly one characterized by abundance and mobility, influence (i.e., persuasion, suggestion) is much more apt to be the process for obtaining consent than is the use of authority. Necessarily, this requires attention to the value systems of subordinates.

Although the leadership in the business firm is, in this sense, subject to constraints, often these will be redundant. That is, the head of the organization will not find it in the least bit constraining to make his choices from a subset known to be acceptable to his subordinates. Particularly in a firm where promotions come from within, the emergence of the chief executive may be largely due to the fact that his value system is a representative one among his associates. Taking into consideration the value conditioning aspect of life in an organization together

---

[11] Actually, Papandreou appears to have in mind all of the members of the coalition—management and nonmanagement alike—whereas I am concerned only with the management group and treat the demands of others as constraints.

with the bilateral screening-selection processes, it is not surprising that the "dictator" should voluntarily be a benevolent one indeed.

Using a benevolent dictatorship assumption, the models employed in Chapter 4 for obtaining the equilibrium and comparative statics responses of the firm handle the social choice problem without any need for modification.

3.4.2. The "Foundation" Model. Casting the managerial discretion model in the framework of Marschak's foundation requires that the management group be able to establish a complete ordering over its alternatives. This does not require identical preference functions among the group members. A degree of uniformity would, however, clearly facilitate such a process. As the preceding discussion indicates, there are substantial grounds for claiming that such a condition exists within the policy-making unit in the business firm.[12]

By restricting our attention to qualitative properties, the details of how the group's utility function is found need not detain us (although it is of some importance that, in principle at least, it is possible). The objective, rather, is to determine whether *all of the qualitative properties of the proposed utility function in Chapter 4 are preserved by treating the firm as a foundation.*

Consider first a two-person management and let the utility function of the firm be represented by

$$W = W(U^1, U^2)$$

where W = utility function of the firm

U^i = utility function of individual i, $i = 1, 2$

and

$$U^i = U^i(Y_1, Y_2, Y_3)$$

where $Y_1 = S$ = staff

$Y_2 = M$ = emoluments

$Y_3 = (1 - t)(R - C - S - M) - \pi_0$ = discretionary profit

---

[12] The remarks of March and Simon on group uniformities are relevant here. They observe that "the utility functions of fairly broad classes of people are very nearly the same; within a given subculture we do not expect radical differences in values. Also, we can expect that if an increase in a given inducement produces an increase in utility for one individual, it will produce an increase for other individuals" [81, p. 87]. Since the managerial discretion model applies to a reasonably homogeneous group in the organization, namely the management, these remarks are applicable to this problem.

First-order conditions for an extremum are obtained by setting the first partials of W with respect to X, S, and M equal to zero. Thus we have

$$(1) \quad \frac{\partial W}{\partial X} = \frac{\partial W}{\partial U^1} \left(\frac{\partial U^1}{\partial Y_1} \frac{\partial Y_1}{\partial X} + \frac{\partial U^1}{\partial Y_2} \frac{\partial Y_2}{\partial X} + \frac{\partial U^1}{\partial Y_3} \frac{\partial Y_3}{\partial X} \right)$$

$$+ \frac{\partial W}{\partial U^2} \left(\frac{\partial U^2}{\partial Y_1} \frac{\partial Y_1}{\partial X} + \frac{\partial U^2}{\partial Y_2} \frac{\partial Y_2}{\partial X} + \frac{\partial U^2}{\partial Y_3} \frac{\partial Y_3}{\partial X} \right) = 0$$

Substituting for $\partial Y_1/\partial X$, $\partial Y_2/\partial X$, and $\partial Y_3/\partial X$, their definitional equivalents and letting $U_j^i = \partial U^i/\partial Y_j$ and $W_i = \partial W/\partial U^i$, we have

$$\frac{\partial W}{\partial X} = W_1 \left[U_3^1(1-t) \left(\frac{\partial R}{\partial X} - \frac{\partial C}{\partial X} \right) \right] + W_2 \left[U_3^2(1-t) \left(\frac{\partial R}{\partial X} - \frac{\partial C}{\partial X} \right) \right] = 0$$

which, upon factoring out the term $\left(\dfrac{\partial R}{\partial X} - \dfrac{\partial C}{\partial X} \right)$, reveals that

$$\left(\frac{\partial R}{\partial X} - \frac{\partial C}{\partial X} \right) = 0$$

Hence

$$\frac{\partial R}{\partial X} = \frac{\partial C}{\partial X} \quad \text{Q.E.D.}$$

$$(2) \quad \frac{\partial W}{\partial S} = W_1 \left[U_1^1 + U_3^1(1-t) \left(\frac{\partial R}{\partial S} - 1 \right) \right]$$

$$+ W_2 \left[U_1^2 + U_3^2(1-t) \left(\frac{\partial R}{\partial S} - 1 \right) \right] = 0$$

or, on collecting terms,

$$(W_1 U_1^1 + W_2 U_1^2) + (W_1 U_3^1 + W_2 U_3^2)(1-t) \left(\frac{\partial R}{\partial S} - 1 \right) = 0$$

But $(W_1 U_j^1 + W_2 U_j^2) = \dfrac{\partial W}{\partial Y_j}$

hence $\dfrac{\partial W}{\partial Y_1} + \dfrac{\partial W}{\partial Y_3}(1-t) \left(\dfrac{\partial R}{\partial S} - 1 \right) = 0$

So
$$\frac{\partial R}{\partial S} = \frac{(-\partial W/\partial Y_1) + (1 - t)(\partial W/\partial Y_3)}{(1 - t)(\partial W/\partial Y_3)}$$

and since $\partial W/\partial Y_j > 0$, all j

$$\frac{\partial R}{\partial S} < 1 \quad \text{Q.E.D.}$$

(3) $\quad \dfrac{\partial W}{\partial M} = W_1[U_2^1 - (1 - t)U_3^1] + W_2[U_2^2 - (1 - t)U_3^2] = 0$

or, on collecting terms,

$$(W_1 U_2^1 + W_2 U_2^2) = (1 - t)(W_1 U_3^1 + W_2 U_3^2)$$

But
$$(W_1 U_j^1 + W_2 U_j^2) = \frac{\partial W}{\partial Y_j}$$

hence
$$\frac{\partial W}{\partial Y_2} = (1 - t)\frac{\partial W}{\partial Y_3}$$

that is, M is chosen so as to maintain a positive proportional relationship between $\partial W/\partial Y_2$ and $\partial W/\partial Y_3$, which is the two-person counterpart for the result of Chapter 4. Q.E.D.

More generally, the model can be cast in terms of an n-person management. Thus, let

$$W = W(U^1, U^2, \ldots, U^i, \ldots, U^n)$$

where $U^i = U^i(Y_1, Y_2, Y_3)$, $i = 1, 2, \ldots, n$.

By collecting terms and simplifying the expressions in the same way as indicated above, the same first-order results obtain. These can be summarized as follows:

Original Model

(4) $\quad \dfrac{\partial R}{\partial X} = \dfrac{\partial C}{\partial X}$

(5) $\quad \dfrac{\partial R}{\partial S} = \dfrac{(-\partial U/\partial Y_1) + (1 - t)(\partial U/\partial Y_3)}{(1 - t)(\partial U/\partial Y_3)} < 1$

(6) $\quad \dfrac{\partial U}{\partial Y_2} = (1 - t)\dfrac{\partial U}{\partial Y_3}$

"Foundation" Adaptation

$$(4') \qquad \frac{\partial R}{\partial X} = \frac{\partial C}{\partial X}$$

$$(5') \qquad \frac{\partial R}{\partial S} = \frac{(-\partial W/\partial Y_1) + (1 - t)(\partial W/\partial Y_3)}{(1 - t)(\partial W/\partial Y_3)} < 1$$

$$(6') \qquad \frac{\partial W}{\partial Y_2} = (1 - t)\frac{\partial W}{\partial Y_3}$$

Since

$$\frac{\partial W}{\partial Y_j} = \frac{\partial W}{\partial U^1}\frac{\partial U^1}{\partial Y_j} + \frac{\partial W}{\partial U^2}\frac{\partial U^2}{\partial Y_j} + \cdots + \frac{\partial W}{\partial U^n}\frac{\partial U^n}{\partial Y_j}$$

we see that the expressions on the right take into account both the "weight" to be assigned to each individual as well as the individual tastes. That is,

$$\frac{\partial W}{\partial U^i} = \text{weight of the } i\text{th managers opinion in the firm}[13]$$

$$\frac{\partial U^i}{\partial Y_j} = \text{intensity of the preference of the } i\text{th manager}$$
$$\text{for the } j\text{th component in } U.$$

Obtaining the comparative statics results proceeds in exactly the same way as indicated in Chapter 4 and with the same results. Thus the foundation assumptions provide results, both for the two-person and for the n-person management, that preserve all of the qualitative characteristics of the managerial discretion model obtained in Chapter 4.

3.4.3. Decentralized Organizations. Many large business firms operate under a highly decentralized form of organization. In this case, a "head-

---

[13] Weights of this sort appear to be what Horwicz had in mind when he observed that "one of the characteristics of any coordinated social enterprise is that conflicts may occur among the desires of various members about the course of their joint activity. To resolve such conflicts, organizations frequently develop rules according to which the desire of each member is assigned some legitimate weight. Each member's weighted desire can then be reckoned up to arrive at a decision which will be binding for the group. The weight assigned to any member's desire may be viewed as that member's legitimate power in the group" [65, p. 166].

quarters" group is assigned the responsibility of coordinating the efforts of a number of largely autonomous "profit centers." In performing this task the headquarters group is typically restricted to laying down guidelines and negotiating "acceptable" operating results[14]—unless, of course, the decentralized operating unit has accumulated a record of what are widely recognized as "blunders." As long, however, as the decentralized unit performs acceptably, it retains considerable autonomy.[15]

For such decentralized firms, the utility function might be interpreted as applying to each of the operating divisions individually. In effect, the headquarters unit distributes the minimum profit constraint imposed on the firm as a whole over the operating divisions and then monitors their progress.[16] The individual divisions can thus be viewed as maximizing their utility, subject to the headquarters-imposed profit constraint.

The components that enter into their separate utility functions are identically those that appear in the utility function given in Chapter 4— with the exception that they are subscripted to reflect the division's activity rather than that of the firm as a whole. The arguments for using the benevolent dictatorship or foundation assumptions are the same as those given above. Thus, all of the qualitative results obtained in Chapter 4 again apply to the decentralized organization.

Whether, for predictive purposes, it is necessary to use a divisional model will largely depend on the nature of the firm's product line. If the entire line is generally responsive to the same market influences, the aggregate model should prove satisfactory. However, where the product line is highly diverse and subject to distinctly different environmental influences, the divisional model may be required.[17]

---

[14] See the discussion in Chapter 6 for details of this process.

[15] Rothenberg suggests that this same phenomenon occurs in the family: as long as an individual performs his specialized decision-making task in an acceptable fashion he is permitted to continue. "Only after frequent gross 'blunders' is complaint likely to take on the complexion of challenge to the prevailing decision-making rules of the game" [98, p. 314].

[16] Transmitting the profit goals to the divisions will involve a certain amount of negotiation with the division managers, as an effort is made to tailor the objective to the separate characteristics of each division. Thus, not all divisions would be assigned the same profit goal. Divisions which have been profit producers in the past will typically be expected to be profit producers in the future, whereas divisions which have been less profitable will be assigned lower profit goals.

[17] The General Manufacturing Company, as reported in Chapter 6, is an example of a firm where the divisional model is essential.

4. Conclusion

In concluding the discussion of the social choice question, the remarks made by Fallding in his review of functional analysis in sociology are perhaps appropriate. Thus, he observes,

> Stability is only secured in social arrangements if everyone [who] is involved in them is "satisfied with them"—at the very least "prepared to put up with them." Everyone must have his reward or the guarantee of it. *Thus the maintenance of stability is essentially a matter of the enlistment of motives. While every person's reward will not be the same, everyone will have the same expectation of a certain reward and hence share a positive regard for, or valuation of, the arrangements* .... [Indeed], value-consensus is the basis of social order .... Where this is lacking in even a single individual there will be disorganization in some degree, however localized. His guarantee of reward is the individual's security, and conformity to the arrangements of the group is what he will give in return for the security gained. In this lies the group's power of control ... and the insurance of its own organization [46, p. 10]. (Italics added.)

Although he does not express his views in terms of the "foundation" conditions of Marschak's that I have found convenient, clearly his argument suggests such an approach.

Treated in all its generality, the social choice question leads to considerable frustration. It can be ignored, but the analysis thereby becomes subject to criticism for failing to consider it. Or it can be mentioned as a factor that limits the generality of the results in some unspecified way, but this is also unsatisfactory. Rather than become entangled in this dilemma, a different course has been pursued. I have argued that the existence of institutional uniformities permit the proposed utility function to accommodate the social choice problem at the level of relevance—albeit at the expense of generality—and proceeded to perform the accommodation. In the process, some suggestions concerning the influence of selection and socialization processes in the business firm have been advanced.

CHAPTER 9

Concluding Remarks

The twin assumptions of self-interest seeking and rationality occupy an important place in economic theory. The first of these is responsible for enormous simplifications in the structure of the behavioral assumptions. Although it requires a specification of what constitutes self-interest, in well-defined situations there frequently appears to be substantial agreement on what objectives have positive content and hence would enhance individual satisfaction. With respect to managerial behavior, the matrix of objectives on page 30 constitutes one such consensus. The assumption of rationality assures that self-interest seeking will proceed efficiently. Together they provide a powerful combination with which to examine economic behavior.

Based on these two assumptions, a general approach for introducing managerial objectives into a theory of the firm has been advanced. This has proceeded in three phases. First, a revision in the character of the motivational assumptions to reflect self-interest seeking was performed. A mathematical model was then fitted to this proposed set of behavioral assumptions and the equilibrium and comparative statics properties of the system were obtained using a maximizing assumption. Finally, evidence bearing on the validity of the theory was examined. We are now in a position to review the analysis. A brief summary is given in Section 1. Some remarks concerning the implications of the analysis for economic policy are given in Section 2. Directions for additional research are indicated in Section 3.

1. A Summary of the Analysis

1.1. On Motivation. Although the managerial discretion models
proposed are derived from what would appear to be a more realistic set
of behavioral assumptions than is the classical theory of the firm, obviously there are influences that have been neglected. Considering, however,
the very limited way that the economic behavior of managers has been
treated previously, the proposed formulation represents a considerable
extension. Self-interest seeking is a well-honored assumption in economics
and it has the distinct advantage of being both fundamental and simple.
Since it is expedient to keep the models simple at this point, this was
felt to be a reasonable approximation.

It is one thing to suggest a more "realistic" set of assumptions. It is
another to reduce these to a form that can be handled analytically. The
essential connection that is introduced for this purpose is that of *expense
preference*. Not only is this notion valuable to the present analysis, but
it would appear to have general relevance in any subsequent efforts to
extend the theory of the firm. Indeed, that so many suggestions for
revision have terminated short of a formal model may be largely attribu-
table to the failure to perceive how expense preference could be used to
connect motives with economic behavior.

Economists have sometimes indicated a certain reluctance to move
their theories in the direction of greater realism in the motivational
assumptions and have emphasized that the real test of a theory rests on
its implications.[1] That is, the test of a theory is whether it renders more
accurate and more numerous implications than do alternative constructions. Certainly this is an unobjectionable criterion. However, it is not
always appreciated that to dismiss the motivational assumptions with an
as if statement may conceal an important set of implications that could
be obtained if the assumptions were formulated with more care. Thus,
it is always possible to say that the firm is operated *as if* to maximize
an objective function that has as principal components Y_1, Y_2, and Y_3
and to proceed from there to a statement of the equilibrium and comparative statics properties of the model. However, such an approach is
hardly apt to promote confidence in the analysis, does not exhaust all
of the implications of the theory, and is unlikely to suggest ways for
modifying or extending the theory.

As was pointed out in Chapter 5, a theory ordinarily has implications
on two levels. First, it has implications for "general behavior." For the

---

[1] Friedman [50, pp. 3–43] is the outstanding advocate of this position.

theory of the firm, these take the form of equilibrium and comparative statics properties. In addition, a theory has implications for "particular behavior"; for example, that differences in competition in the product market and differences in tastes between managements have a systematic influence on the way in which resources are distributed within the organization. Whereas implications for general behavior can be deduced from an *as if* statement of the hypothesis, implications for particular behavior rely on a deliberate motivation of the theory. They rest on a *weltanschauung* that provides a frame of reference with which to digest observations across a wide range of phenomena that are not comprehended by the formal model alone.[2] Hence, to express the motivational assumptions in an *as if* fashion may conceal an important class of behavior upon which the theory can be made to render predictions. The retained earnings analysis reported in Chapter 7 is an example of precisely this sort. It would be missed entirely by an isolated statement of the hypothesis that the firm is operated *as if* to maximize the utility function

$$U = U[S, M, (1 - t)(R - C - S - M) - \pi_0]$$

1.2. On Managerial Models. The truism that individuals typically derive satisfaction in a variety of ways has been generally neglected in the theory of the firm. This may be due to a pervasive belief that "it is much harder to derive operationally meaningful theorems concerning firm behavior from a construction ... directly based on preference-function maximization than ... from the profit maximization construction" [92, p. 211]. It is my contention that this is only partly correct. In the mechanical sense of manipulating symbols to derive meaningful theorems, the managerial discretion models proposed are indeed more awkward to handle than are either of the profit maximization models examined. Appendices 4-A and 4-B explicitly reveal the nature of the difficulties. Computational difficulties aside, however, the preference function constructions proposed were, after modest qualifications (e.g., disallowing any of the components in the utility functions to be treated as an inferior good), shown to yield testable implications. Thus, in order for the quotation cited above to be fully accurate, the preference functions mentioned should be referred to as *"completely general* preference functions." With this stipulation, preference function analyses of the sort proposed here would be largely defeated. But, as I have argued in Chapter 4, although such a stipulation is appropriate to the general analysis

---

[2] For an interesting comparison of mathematical and verbal models and their relative advantages see [116].

of consumer behavior, it is unwarranted in the context of the specific models under investigation here. Where we are dealing with specific problems we are entitled to modest specializations. If this is granted, then preference function constructions need not render the theory void of implications. In this sense, which is clearly the most important one, the quotation cited above exaggerates the difficulties.

The managerial discretion models proposed preserve the main theorems of the profit maximization hypothesis with respect to shifts in demand and the application of a sales tax of either the specific or ad valorem variety. Indeed, since there is little dispute concerning the general validity of these implications of the classical theory, it would be distressing to have the discretion models predict differently. However, when it comes to matters where the qualitative implications of the profit maximizing model have been suspect, namely the effects of a profits tax and a lump-sum tax, the discretion models register responses that contradict the classical theory. They therefore provide theoretical support to some of those who have argued on empirical grounds that the implications of the classical theory, with respect to these tax effects, are incorrect.[3]

Two interesting mathematical properties of the managerial discretion models were developed in Appendices 4-A and 4-B. The first of these shows that the so-called Fundamental Equation of Value Theory (from the analysis of consumer behavior) can be applied to a theory of the firm restructured in the way I have suggested.[4] Thus the effect of a change in the profits tax rate can be separated into a net substitution effect (which is always positive with respect to staff and emoluments) and an income effect (which is always negative). The gross substitution effect, which is probably positive, is a combination of these two separate effects.

Appendix 4-B shows that Lancaster's recent characterization of the scope of qualitative economics [77] can be extended somewhat. Where sign relationships fail to yield unambiguous predictions, it may frequently be true that replacing the signs by the functional relations that they represent will permit cancellations among some of the terms and thereby lead to determinate results.

---

[3] The issue is by no means resolved. For a review of some of the previous empirical results and for an interesting addition to the debate, see [75].

[4] Graaff has used the notion of the "income effect" in proposing a revision in the concept of the entrepreneur [55]. He treats the entrepreneur as a consumer who maximizes his utility subject to budgetary and transformation (i.e., production) function constraints. He argues that an increase in the price of a factor may lead to an increase in its employment due to pressure on the entrepreneur to work harder, expand his operations, and offset the added cost through added revenue [55, p. 82].

The social choice question was examined in Chapter 8. It was argued that the impossibility of obtaining completely general social welfare functions that meet all the axioms of desirability does not render all attempts at aggregating individual preferences hopeless. In well-defined groups there is usually agreement on the mechanism for obtaining a decision as well as a substantial value consensus among the membership. In these circumstances, an autocratic or benevolent dictatorship model or, more generally, a foundation model (as defined by Marschak) may lead to a social welfare function that does not violate any of the essential group choice processes in the organization under study. This is particularly likely in the top ranks of an organization, such as a business firm, where the membership is sequentially screened and a socialization process applied to its values. The argument may well be transferable to other social choice situations where inherent group stability processes, which would legitimately permit the analysis to be specialized, have been neglected in favor of the abstract objective of generality.

1.3. On the Evidence. Taken individually, the results from each of the field studies and principal firm tests tend to support the managerial discretion model. The evidence suggests that managerial objectives have a systematic influence on the operations of the firm, and that conditions of competition in the product market play a critical role in determining the extent to which discretionary behavior is quantitatively important. Collectively, the results are even more compelling. Whereas "no single bit of evidence or no single line of argument is sufficient 'to prove beyond a reasonable doubt,' ... the combined evidence makes the conclusion highly probable" [31, p. 349].

Although to use the phrase "highly probable" to characterize the results at this point is an overstatement, surely it is not too much to claim that doubt has been cast on the proposition that managerial objectives are unimportant. By employing the notion of *expense preference* the economist can provide nonpecuniary motives with economic content. As Becker has observed, "progress in this field has been hindered not so much by an intractable concept as by the economists' reluctance to take the concept seriously" [14, p. 179].

The evidence gathered in the field studies emphasized operating rules and operating behavior, rather than opinion, as the basis for evaluating the business behavior. Although "reasonableness" arguments had to be invoked in evaluating the field study evidence, these were performed with some care. First, the observations are subject to *ceteris paribus* interpretations. To minimize these difficulties, the field studies were restricted to those of the "extreme instance" variety. Second, the quantitative responses had to be provided with an interpretative framework. A general model for evaluating the gross characteristics of the quantitative responses was devised for this purpose. Hence, if differences over the interpretation of the evidence arise, these probably can be traced back to differences in the mechanisms that are perceived to be operating. Third, a question of relating the observations to intent arose. To help to answer this requirement, the numerical data were supplemented by descriptions of the processes that the firms employed to achieve the results. Finally, the issue of generality was treated by indicating that the business literature appears to abound with observations of a similar, if less extensive, kind. In general, the managerial discretion model appears to fit the data moderately well.

The results from the principal firm tests, although preliminary, suggest that the conditions of discretion (and possibly the tastes of the management for personal satisfaction) have a definite effect on the operations of the business firm. Moreover, the tests of racial and religious discrimination reported by Becker [12], although not explicitly concerned with any of the issues I raise, are clearly concerned with a similar type of question: namely, does the condition of competition in the product market influence discretionary expenditures within the firm? His results, like mine, confirm this hypothesis and thus lend additional support to this general position.

2. Implications for Economic Policy

Baumol has argued that firms that maximize sales subject to a profit constraint will produce more than they would if operated as profit maximizers [11, pp. 76–77].[5] As a result, the undesirable resource allocation results generally attributed to firms that possess a degree of monopoly power may vanish. As Baumol observes, "distortions [from ideal output] may tend roughly to cancel out" [11, p. 77].

Firms that maximize a utility function of the form I have specified will also expand output beyond the profit maximizing level. However, an important difference between the sales maximization and the utility maximization models exists. In the former, a general expansion in the

---

[5] Although Shepherd has indicated that this result may require qualification [107], it would appear to be generally correct.

scale of operations occurs; in the latter, expansion occurs only as a result of the positive preference for staff, and the output response is derived rather than direct. Rather than expand the scale of operations generally from the profit maximizing position (as occurs in the sales maximizing firm), the expansion favors hierarchical expense and output is increased only to the level where the marginal costs of production are brought into equality with the marginal gross revenue at this higher level of staff expense (see Figure 1 in Chapter 4). If increasing staff tends to make the demand curve progressively more inelastic as it shifts the demand curve to the right,[6] increases in price rather than increases in output may characterize the discretion model. Hence, a less desirable welfare result than Baumol was inclined to associate with the sales maximization hypothesis would obtain. Indeed, if cost asymmetries are important and expansionary objectives show up largely in prices rather than output, the effect of monopoly on efficiency can scarcely be dismissed.

Measures designed to increase the amount of price competition in the product market necessarily reduce these asymmetries. By pressing the firm more severely, staff, emoluments, and price can all be expected to yield. Conceivably the effect on technological progress may be adverse, but this is an open question.[7] Moreover, whichever way it is resolved, the efficiency effects suggested by the discretion model continue to be important for purposes of evaluating alternative economic arrangements. With respect to international trade, for example, tariff reductions may be valued for the stimulus to competition that these provide in addition to their effects on international resource allocation. The recent surge of the French economy has been attributed in part to precisely the change in the competitive climate associated with the development of the European Economic Community [33].

If a systematic accumulation of staff and emoluments occurs during prosperity, while a divestment frequently becomes necessary during adversity, expense preference behavior might be expected to accentuate the business cycle. However this remark requires qualification in two senses. First, although firms that display a positive preference for hierarchical expense may make sizeable adjustments in these expenditures

---

[6] That is, the effects of increasing general administrative and selling expense may essentially be to develop strong and stable product preference relations. Thus expenditures on advertising, customer services, expense accounts, product differentiation, etc., could all tend to make demand for the firm's products more inelastic.

[7] See Mansfield [80] for a general review of the arguments on each side of this issue.

in response to changes in business conditions, these will be of a character that tend to moderate fluctuations in reported profits and hence the income stream from this source will be stabilized. Second, firms that possess considerable discretion may delay their responses in the hope that an improvement will develop. Hence, in mild recessions they may scarcely respond at all and thus could moderate rather than accentuate the cyclical adjustment. The effects thus appear to be somewhat mixed. Whereas firms that possess discretion in industries that are severely affected by a business decline could be expected to make sharp cutbacks in hierarchical expense, those in industries less affected may adjust hardly at all. And although expense preference behavior will tend to reduce the level of average profits, it should also reduce the variance.

The short-run effects of high marginal corporation tax rates that are indicated by the discretion model (as well as by the discounted profit maximization model when these rates are temporary) suggest that the excess profits tax is an inferior tax collection device. Such taxes will be avoided by incurring current costs to absorb current profits. Although some of these expenditures may produce desirable long-run economic benefits, many of them may enhance only short-run individual objectives.

The results of the principal firm analysis are preliminary and may require subsequent revision. At present, however, although the evidence on the effects of internal composition of the board is weak, the implications for selecting members to the board of directors are obvious. Both with respect to executive compensation and dividend policy, management representation on the board appears to subordinate stockholder to managerial interests. The advantage to the stockholders of an independent board is therefore clear. Although Gordon [54, pp. 343–51] and Douglas [42, p. 53] have already argued this case persuasively, the reasoning has lacked empirical support and there is no indication that their views have been heeded. If additional evidence on this matter confirms the findings, the need for such reforms becomes much more compelling.

As a general heuristic for using economic theory to assist in economic policy formation, it may be useful to partition the universe according to some generally accepted criterion and then assign models to the sectors that they characterize best. One class of models would be used in one sector, a second class of models in a second sector, and so forth. An initial partitioning into competitive and monopolistic sectors would probably be sufficient. Within the competitive sector, the long-period profit maximizing model that was proposed in Chapter 5 may often be the most useful construction. For purposes of studying behavior in the monopoly sector where conditions of discretion frequently prevail, the discretion models may often be the most appropriate:[8] they provide a fruitful and orderly way with which to structure a broad range of monopoly practices. Indeed, to neglect managerial objectives in the analysis of this sector may be to require *ad hoc* explanations for behavior that is entirely rational and hence subject to systematic analysis and routine explanation.

Although the monopolistic sector probably represents somewhat less than one-third of the economic activity in the United States [90, p. 20] [121, p. 50], it is a very conspicuous sector. It includes most of the highly visible industries (steel, electrical equipment, automobiles, cigarettes, and so forth) and draws far more political attention than does the more sizeable competitive sector. Whether this attention is warranted is not the issue. As long as the monopolistic sector is a politically interesting one, a model explicitly designed to explain the discretion that is associated with the larger "opportunity sets" that exist in this sector is clearly suggested.

In the very long run, of course, the special advantages that insulate a firm from the pressures of competition tend to be eroded and may fail to be replaced by others. Hence, discretion that exists in the short run may disappear as the time period is extended. Thus, where the interest is in predicting the eventual rather than the current response of the firm, the profit maximizing model may enjoy a general advantage in both competitive and monopolistic sectors.[9] For many policy purposes, how-

---

[8] Being a heuristic, the partitioning is only suggestive rather than definitive. It leaves open the possibility of using the short-period profit maximizing model in the competitive sector for some purposes, of using the long-period profit maximizing model in the monopolistic sector in other circumstances, and so forth. In general, however, the heuristic should prove useful and deviations from it, for reasons other than simplicity, would appear to warrant separate justification. Where implications among the several models are *overlapping*, however, simplicity may constitute an adequate justification itself. For example, in studying the qualitative response of staff and output to a shift in demand, the short-run profit maximization model would appear to be appropriate across both of the sectors.

[9] Since completing the dissertation I have further elaborated my views on the time horizon for which the managerial discretion models are appropriate. Taking the short run to be somewhat less than two years, the intermediate run as two to five years, and the long run as over five years, I would suggest that the Cyert and March "behavioral theory of the firm" [38, Chap. 8] type of model be used in the short run, the managerial discretion models or similar partial equilibrium models (such as Baumol's sales maximization hypothesis [11]) be used in the intermediate run in circumstances where competition in the product market is not typically severe, the discounted profit maximization partial equilibrium model proposed in Chapter 5 be used in the intermediate run where competition in the product market is vigorous, and a general equilibrium version of the profit maximization construction be used in the long run. Although the rules under which the thesis was selected for publication preclude a full elaboration of the argument, details can be found in [130].

ever, the short-run response is frequently the overriding consideration. Proposals to stimulate the economy during recessions and to contain the economy during a boom by flexible use of tax policy at least appear to fall in this category as, indeed, do similar suggestions with respect to depreciation policy, investment credits, and so forth. For such purposes the managerial discretion models (or similar constructions) may well be of critical importance.

3. Some Directions for Future Research

Among possible subjects for future research are the following:

1. Labor economists have frequently used concentration and unionization ratios to explain the wage structure [22] [52]. This suggests that the labor sector may capture some fraction of monopoly profits. In studying this question in more detail, however, specific attention to the skill mix and a separation of short-run from long-run effects may be essential.

2. A dynamic version of the model that preserves the essential properties of the static analysis may produce additional testable propositions. For example, Bonini has used a computer model to show that cyclical fluctuations with high amplitude lead to higher average profits than occurs with the same mean but lower amplitude. He characterizes this as "the most significant effect in the study" [20, pp. 166–68]. This same result can be obtained by an adaptation of the present model by permitting the firm to encounter its minimum profit constraint when the amplitude is great but not otherwise. Increasing the frequency of the cycles would also produce higher average performance if it were assumed that the firm responds more quickly to adversity than prosperity. In addition, the evidence in Chapter 6 suggests that there may be systematic differences in the sequence with which particular expenses are adjusted. These could also be made a part of a dynamic model.

3. The aggregation problem has yet to be handled. Certain simplifications will be necessary for such a purpose. For example, the analysis would be facilitated by assuming characteristic uniformities throughout the industry. Although some difficulties may be encountered, I see no reason why the usual result obtained from models that assume rational behavior would be violated—namely, that the market response is merely the "macro-version of an individual's response" [13, p. 13].

4. Although the analysis has examined the tax question more sharply than previous treatments, the real test is an empirical one. An econometric model will be necessary for such purposes. In addition, there are a variety of tests of particular behavior that are suggested by the analysis. If my contention that the self-interest seeking assumption can be fruitfully applied to the analysis of managerial behavior is essentially correct, it leads to rational interpretations of a variety of phenomena that are treated as peculiarities by previous constructions.

5. The evidence in Chapters 6 and 7 raises a serious question as to whether studies of monopoly power based on reported profit[10] provide an accurate estimate of the effects of monopoly. It is possible that a nonnegligible part of true monopoly profit is absorbed internally. A continuing investigation of these effects would appear to be warranted.

---

[10] Harberger's analysis of the effects of monopoly [61] employs the reported profit measure. Although Schwartzman [101], comes to conclusions similar to Harberger's without using reported profit in this way, his conclusions are subject to question on the issue of representativeness in his sample.

Bibliography *

1. Alchian, A. A., "Uncertainty, Evolution, and Economic Theory," *Journal of Political Economy*, June 1950, **58**, 211–21.

2. ———, and R. A. Kessel, "Competition, Monopoly, and the Pursuit of Pecuniary Gain," in *Aspects of Labor Economics*. Princeton: National Bureau of Economic Research, 1962.

3. Allen, R. G. D., *Mathematical Economics*. 2nd ed., London: St. Martin's Press, 1959.

4. Archibald, G. C., "The State of Economic Science" (Review), *British Journal for the Philosophy of Science*, May 1959, **10**, 58–69.

5. Arrow, K. J., *Social Choice and Individual Values*. New York: John Wiley & Sons, Inc., 1951.

6. Averch, H. and L. L. Johnson, "Behavior of the Firm Under Regulatory Constraint," *American Economic Review*, December 1962, **52**, 1052–69.

7. Bain, J. S., *Barriers to New Competition*. Cambridge: Harvard University Press, 1956.

8. ———, *Industrial Organization*. New York: John Wiley & Sons, Inc., 1959.

9. Barnard, C. I., *The Functions of the Executive*. Cambridge, 1962.

10. ———, "Functions and Pathology of Status Systems in Formal Organizations," in *Industry and Society* (W. F. Whyte, ed.). New York: McGraw-Hill, Inc., 1946.

---

* The bibliography includes only those works that have been referred to in the text and footnotes. Materials that were examined in the preparation of the thesis but not cited are therefore omitted. For an extensive bibliography of the theory of the firm literature, see Bowen [20]. March and Simon [77] provide a bibliography to the organization theory literature. Citations to the social choice question can be found in Rothenberg [93].

11. Baumol, W. J., *Business Behavior, Value, and Growth.* New York: The Macmillan Company, 1959.

12. Becker, G. S., *The Economics of Discrimination.* Chicago: University of Chicago Press, 1957.

13. Becker, G. S., "Irrational Behavior and Economic Theory," *Journal of Political Economy,* February 1962, **70,** 1–13.

14. ———, "Competition, Monopoly, and the Pursuit of Monopoly Gain: Comment," in *Aspects of Labor Economics.* Princeton: National Bureau of Economic Research, 1962.

15. ———, "A Reply to A. Kirzner," *Journal of Political Economy,* February 1963, **71,** 82–83.

16. Behavioral Sciences Subpanel, President's Science Advisory Committee, *Strengthening the Behavioral Sciences.* Washington, D. C., 1962.

17. Bergson, A., "A Reformulation of Certain Aspects of Welfare Economics," *Quarterly Journal of Economics,* February 1938, **52,** 233–52.

18. Berle, A. A. and G. C. Means, *The Modern Corporation and Private Property.* New York: Commerce Clearing House, Inc., 1932.

19. Black, D., *The Theory of Committees and Elections.* London: Cambridge University Press, 1958.

20. Bonini, C. P., *Simulation of Information and Decision Systems in the Firm,* unpublished Doctor's Dissertation, Carnegie Institute of Technology, 1962.

21. Boulding, K. E., "Implications for General Economics of More Realistic Theories of the Firm," *American Economic Review,* May 1952, **42,** 30–44.

22. Bowen, H. R., *The Business Enterprise as a Subject for Research,* prepared for the Committee of Business Research (Pamphlet 11). New York: Social Science Research Council, 1955.

23. Bowen, W. G., *Wage Behavior in the Postwar Period,* Princeton: Princeton University Press, 1960.

24. Bresciani-Turroni, C., *The Economics of Inflation.* London, 1937.

25. Bridgman, P. W., *The Logic of Modern Physics.* New York: The Macmillan Company, 1927.

26. Brim, O. G., D. C. Glass, D. E. Lavin, and N. Goodman, *Personality and Decision Processes*. Stanford: Stanford University Press, 1962.

27. Bronfenbrenner, M., "Competition, Monopoly, and the Pursuit of Pecuniary Gain: Comment," in *Aspects of Labor Economics*. Princeton: National Bureau of Economic Research, 1962.

28. Cagan, P., "The Monetary Dynamics of Hyperinflation," in *Studies in the Quantity Theory of Money*. Chicago, 1956.

29. Cartwright, D. and A. Zander, *Group Dynamics: Research and Theory*. 2nd ed. New York: Harper & Row, Publishers, 1960.

30. Cochran, W. G., *Sampling Techniques*. New York: John Wiley & Sons, Inc., 1953.

31. Cohen, M. R. and E. Nagel, *An Introduction to Logic and Scientific Method*. New York: Harcourt, Brace & World, Inc., 1935.

32. Cole, A. H., *Business Enterprise in its Social Setting*. Cambridge: Harvard University Press, 1959.

33. *Communanté Européenne*, January 1963, cited by D. Cordtz in "France Rides High" [36].

34. Cooper, W. W., "Theory of the Firm—Some Suggestions for Revision," *American Economic Review*, December 1949, **39**, 1204–22.

35. ———, "The Current State of Managerial Economics," *American Economic Review*, May 1961, **51**, 131–41.

36. Cordtz, D., "France Rides High," *The Wall Street Journal*, February 1, 1963.

37. Cournot, A., *Researches into the Mathematical Principles of the Theory of Wealth*, 1897. (Trans. N. T. Bacon). New York: The Macmillan Company, 1927.

38. Cyert, R. M. and J. G. March, *A Behavioral Theory of the Firm*. Englewood Cliffs, N. J.: Prentice-Hall, Inc., 1963.

39. Cyert, R. M. and E. Grunberg, "Assumption, Prediction, and Explanation in Economics," Appendix A of A Behavioral Theory of the Firm [38].

40. Dibble, V. K., "Occupations and Ideologies," *American Journal of Sociology*, September 1962, **68**, 229–41.

41. Dorfman, R., "Operations Research," *American Economic Review*, September 1960, **50**, 575–623.

42. Douglas, W. O., *Democracy in Finance*. New Haven: Yale University Press, 1940.

43. Eckstein, O. and T. A. Wilson, "The Determination of Money Wages in American Industry," *Quarterly Journal of Economics*, August 1962, **76**, 379–414.

44. Edwards, C. D., "Conglomerate Bigness as a Source of Power," in *Business Concentration and Price Policy*. Princeton: Princeton University Press, 1955.

45. Ellsberg, D., "Classic and Current Notions of "Measurable Utility,' " *Economic Journal*, September, 1954, **64**, 528–56.

46. Fallding, H., "Functional Analysis in Sociology," *American Sociological Review*, February 1963, **28**, 5–18.

47. Festinger, L., "Informed Social Communication," *Psychological Review*, 1950, **57**, 271–82.

48. Friedman, J. J., "Top Management Faces the Cost Challenge," *Dun's Review and Modern Industry*, January 1961, **77**, 34–36.

49. Friedman, M., "Prices, Income, and Monetary Changes in Three Wartime Periods," *American Economic Review*, May 1952, **42**, 612–25.

50. ———, *Essays in Positive Economics*. Chicago: University of Chicago Press, 1953.

51. ———, *A Program for Monetary Stability*. New York: Fordham University Press, 1960.

52. Garbarino, J. W., "A Theory of Interindustry Wage Structure Variation," *Quarterly Journal of Economics*, May 1950, **64**, 282–305.

53. Gordon, M. J., *The Investment, Financing, and Valuation of the Corporation*. Homewood, Ill.: Richard D. Irwin, Inc., 1962.

54. Gordon, R. A., *Business Leadership in the Large Corporation*. Berkeley: University of California Press, 1961.

55. Graaff, J. de V., "Income Effects and the Theory of the Firm," *Review of Economic Studies*, 1950–51, **18**, 79–86.

56. ———, *Theoretical Welfare Economics*. London: Cambridge University Press, 1957.

57. ———, "On Making a Recommendation in a Democracy," *Economic Journal*, June 1962, **72**, 293–300.

58. Grunberg, E., "Notes on the Verifiability of Economic Laws," *Philosophy of Science*, October 1957, **24**, 337–48.

59. Haire, M., "Psychological Problems Relevant to Business and Industry," *Psychological Bulletin*, May 1959, **56**, 169–94.

60. Hammer, R., "Why Things Went Sour for Louis Wolfson," *Fortune*, September 1961, **64**, 132–34.

61. Harberger, A. C., "Monopoly and Resource Allocation," *American Economic Review*, May 1954, **44**, 75–87.

62. Hempel, C. G. and P. Oppenheim, "Studies in the Logic of Explanation," *Philosophy of Science*, January 1948, **15**, 135–78.

63. Hicks, J. R., "Annual Survey of Economic Theory: The Theory of Monopoly," *Econometrica*, January 1935, **3**, 1–20.

64. ———, "Foundations of Welfare Economics," *Economic Journal*, December 1939, **49**, 696–712.

65. Horwicz, M., "Psychological Needs as a Function of Social Environment," in *The State of the Social Sciences* (L. D. White, ed.), Chicago, 1956.

66. Hurwicz, L., "The Theory of the Firm and of Investment," *Econometrica*, April 1946, **14**, 109–36.

67. Johnson, H. M., *Sociology*. New York: Harcourt, Brace & World, Inc., 1960.

68. Kaldor, N., "Welfare Propositions in Economics," *Economic Journal*, September 1939, **49**, 549–52.

69. Kaysen, C., "The Corporation: How Much Power? What Scope?" in *The Corporation in Modern Society* (E. S. Mason, ed.). Cambridge: Harvard University Press, 1960.

70. Katz, R. L., *Executive Teamwork: Coordination in a Medium-Sized Company*. Unpublished Doctoral Dissertation, Harvard University, 1956

71. Keynes, J. M., *Essays in Persuasion*. London: Macmillan & Co., Ltd., 1931.

72. Knauth, O., *Managerial Enterprise: It's Growth and Methods of Operations*. New York: W. W. Norton & Company, Inc., 1948.

73. Koontz, H. and C. O'Donnell, *Principles of Management*. New York: McGraw-Hill, Inc., 1955.

74. Koopmans, T. C., *Three Essays on the State of Economic Science*. New York: McGraw-Hill, Inc., 1957.

75. Kryzyaniak, M. and R. A. Musgrave, *The Shifting of the Corporation Income Tax* (mimeo.), October 1962.

76. Kuhn, H. W. and C. W. Tucker, "Nonlinear Programming," in *Proceedings of the Second Berkeley Symposium on Mathematical Statistics and Probability*. Berkeley: University of California Press, 1951.

77. Lancaster, K. J., "The Scope of Qualitative Economics," *Review of Economic Studies*, January 1962, **29,** 99–123.

78. Luce, R. D. and H. Raiffa, *Games and Decisions*. New York: John Wiley & Sons., Inc., 1957.

79. McGuire, J. W., J. S. Y. Chiu, and A. O. Elbing, "Executive Incomes, Sales, and Profits," *American Economic Review*, September 1962, **52,** 753–61.

80. Mansfield, E., "Size of Firm, Market Structure, and Innovation," *Journal of Political Economy*, December 1963, **71,** 556–76.

81. March, J. G. and H. A. Simon, *Organizations*. New York: John Wiley & Sons., Inc., 1958.

82. Marschak, J., "Towards an Economic Theory of Organization and Information, "in *Decision Processes* (R. M. Thrall, C. H. Coombs, and R. L. Davis, eds.). New York: John Wiley & Sons. Inc., 1954.

83. Marshall, A., *Principles of Economics*. 8th ed., New York: The Macmillan Company, 1948.

84. ———, *Industry and Trade*. London 1932.

85. Maslow, A. H., "A Dynamic Theory of Motivation," *Psychological Review*, July 1943, **50,** 370–96.

86. Mason, E. S. (ed.), *The Corporation in Modern Society*. Cambridge: Harvard University Press, 1960.

87. *Moody's Industrial Manual: 1962* (J. S. Porter, Editor-in-Chief). New York 1962.

88. Moore, W. E., *The Conduct of the Corporation*. New York: Random House, 1962.

89. Musgrave, R. A., *The Theory of Public Finance*. New York: McGraw-Hill, Inc., 1959.

90. Nutter, G. W., *The Extent of Enterprise Monopoly in the United States*. Chicago: University of Chicago Press, 1951.

91. Papandreou, A. G., "Economics and the Social Sciences," *Economic Journal*, December 1950, **60**, 715–23.

92. ———, "Some Basic Issues in the Theory of the Firm," in *A. Survey of Contemporary Economics* (B. F. Haley, ed.). Homewood, Ill.: Richard D. Irwin, Inc., 1952.

93. Pigou, A. C., *The Economics of Welfare*. 4th ed., London: Macmillan & Co., Ltd., 1950.

94. Presthus, R. V., "Authority in Organizations," in *Concepts and Issues in Administrative Behavior*. (S. Mailick and E. H. VonNess, eds.) Englewood Cliffs, N. J.: Prentice-Hall, Inc., 1962.

95. Reder, M. W., "A Reconsideration of the Marginal Productivity Theory," *Journal of Political Economy*, October 1947, **55**, 450–58.

96. Roberts, D. R., *Executive Compensation*. New York: Free Press of Glencoe, Inc., 1959.

97. Rostow, E. V., "To Whom and for What Ends is Corporate Management Responsible?" in *The Corporation in Modern Society* (E. S. Mason, ed.). Cambridge: Harvard University Press, 1960.

98. Rothenberg, J., *The Measurement of Social Welfare*. Englewood Cliffs, N. J.: Prentice-Hall, Inc., 1961.

99. Samuelson, P. A., *Foundations of Economic Analysis*. Cambridge: 1958.

100. ———, "Problems of Methodology: Comment," *American Economic Review*, May 1963, **53**, 231–36.

101. Schwartzman, D., "The Effect of Monopoly on Price," *Journal of Political Economy*, August 1959, **67**, 352–62.

102. Schumpeter, J. A., *Capitalism, Socialism, and Democracy*. 3rd. ed., New York: Harper & Row, Publishers, 1947.

103. Scitovski, T., "A Note on Profit Maximization and Its Implications," *Review of Economic Studies*, 1943, **11**, 57–60.

104. ————, "Economic Theory and the Measurement of Concentration," in *Business Concentration and Price Policy*. Princeton: Princeton University Press, 1955.

105. Scott, R. H., *Debt Management for Economic Stability*. Unpublished Doctor's Dissertation, Harvard University 1961.

106. Scott, M. Fg., "Relative Share Prices and Yields," *Oxford Economic Papers*, N. S., October 1962, **14**, 218–50.

107. Shepherd, W. G., "On Sales-Maximizing and Oligopoly Behavior," *Economica*, N. S., November 1962, **29**, 420–24.

108. Simon, H. A., "A Comparison of Organization Theories," *Review of Economic Studies*, 1952–53, **20**, 40–48.

109. ————, "Rational Behavior and Organization Theory," in *Trends in Economics*, Penn State Univ., University Park, Pa.: Pennsylvania State University Press, 1955.

110. ————, *Models of Man*. New York: John Wiley & Sons, Inc., 1957.

111. ————, "The Compensation of Executives," *Sociometry*, March 1957, **20**, 32–35.

112. ————, "Theories of Decision Making in Economics and Behavioral Science," *American Economic Review*, June 1959, **49**, 253–83.

113. ————, *Administrative Behavior*. 2nd ed., New York 1961.

114. ————, "New Developments in the Theory of the Firm," *American Economic Review*, May 1962, **52**, 1–15.

115. ————, "Problems in Methodology: Comment," *American Economic Review*, May 1963, **53**, 229–31.

116. ————, and A. Newell, "Models: Their Uses and Limitations," in *The State of the Social Sciences* (L. D. White, ed.) Chicago: University of Chicago Press, 1956.

117. Smith, A., *The Wealth of Nations.* Modern Library ed., New York: Modern Library, Inc., 1937.

118. Stagner, R. and T. F. Karwoski, *Psychology.* New York: McGraw-Hill, Inc., 1952.

119. Stedry, A. C., *Budget Control and Cost Behavior.* Englewood Cliffs, N. J.: Prentice-Hall, Inc., 1960.

120. Stigler, G. J., *The Theory of Price.* New York: The Macmillan Company, 1949.

121. ———, *Five Lectures on Economic Problems.* London, 1949.

122. ———, "Industrial Organization and Economic Progress," in *The State of the Social Sciences* (L. D. White, ed.). Chicago: University of Chicago Press, 1956.

123. ———, "The Statistics of Monopoly and Merger," *Journal of Political Economy,* February 1956, **64,** 33–40.

124. Theil, H., "On the Symmetry Approach to the Committee Decision Problem," *Report 6209* (MS No. 16) International Center for Management Science, Netherlands School of Economics, 1962. (mimeo.)

125. Thompson, E. T., "The Cost Cutting Urge," *Fortune,* May 1958, **57,** 118–21.

126. Thompson, V. A., *Modern Organization.* New York: Alfred A. Knopf, Inc., 1961.

127. *The Wall Street Journal,* "White Collar Cutback," January 3, 1963, 1.

128. Williamson, O. E., "Selling Expense as a Barrier to Entry," *Quarterly Journal of Economics,* February 1963, **77,** 112–28.

129. ———, "A Model of Rational Managerial Behavior," Chap. 9 in [38].

130. ———, "Horizons, Assumptions, and the Theory of the Firm," *Working Paper No. 85.* Berkeley: Center for Research in Management Science, University of California, 1963.

131. Winter, S. G., Jr., *Economic Natural Selection and the Theory of the Firm.* Unpublished monograph, 1960.